Endorsements

In more than thirty years of ministry to the poor, we have learned how vital it is to stand firm on the very thing Roland Worton writes about in this book—joy! The supernatural joy that comes not from circumstances, possessions, or reputation, but from the overwhelming, overflowing presence of our Father, shining in the depth of our hearts no matter the labor or season. His presence is the promise of Christ in us, and it has kept us worshipping in true gratitude through more trials than we could ever say. We warmly invite you to join Roland in contemplating this priceless inheritance, and may every page bless you.

HEIDI G. BAKER, PH.D.
Co-founder and Executive Chairman of the Board, Iris Global

The nations are ready and waiting for the Father's joy! *The Surprising Power of Joy* invites us into reclaiming and releasing all that has been made available to us in Jesus. Our lives were forever transformed by the supernatural power of Heaven's joy—and it is still a necessity for us every day. This book will cause you to recapture a hunger to be filled and overflowing, creating culture and an atmosphere that releases the Father's impacting joy. Take it! Receive it! Release it!

GEORGIAN BANOV
President and Co-founder, Global Celebration and GCSSM Online

What a timely and much-needed message! In his book, *The Surprising Power of Joy*, Roland Worton with clarity, precision, and prophetic insight, not only stirs us into a deeper desire and longing for the presence of the Lord, but also reminds us of God's extravagant love and joy for us. I've had the pleasure of knowing Roland for over two decades. The consistency and authenticity of his life and message come from the very place he so masterfully shares with us in this book.

With so much shaking and seeming uncertainties at this critical juncture in the world today, this book is a much-needed resource that reminds us where all lasting joy and power come from. Reading through the pages, I found myself reinvigorated and longing to enjoy resting in the Lord's presence...just because, because, because of who He is and what He has already done. Yes, may you too be reminded of the power of joy unspeakable, love incomprehensible, and peace beyond human understanding as you take devotion time to read through this timely message.

DOUG STRINGER
Founder/President, Somebody Cares America, Somebody Cares International, Turning Point Ministries Int'l. Houston, Texas

Roland Worton's new book, *The Surprising Power of Joy*, has the delightful "Jesus-like" quality of helping people heal. Roland points out how God's Kingdom was designed for joy, as he offers a whole range of ways to be introduced to joy, and provides catalytic challenges to help us discover and experience more joy in countless ways. Roland has a winsome way of presenting profound theological concepts that are easily apprehended. For example, He shows how creation and incarnation demonstrate God's invitation to joy, and His desire to share that joy with us. Roland then shares invitations to nurture joy in our lives. Readers may not have the sense to respond and enter into the joy God has for them, but at least they will have been told that they don't have to live joyless, lackluster lives!

DR. BILL ATWOOD
Anglican Bishop and author of
The General, The Boy, & Recapturing Joy

Roland Worton is one of the most exuberant worshippers and worship leaders I know. I felt this same exuberance while reading *The Surprising Power of Joy*. The Apostle Paul, while writing to the highly persecuted Christians in Rome, describes the atmosphere of God's rulership. One of three words he chooses is *joy!* This book is a timely reminder in a moment where the kingdoms of this world are vying for power that joy is not only an emotion, it is a ruling force of the greater Kingdom of God. I highly recommend this book!

BOB HAZLETT

Author of *The Roar: God's Sound in a Raging World*

www.bobhazlett.org

This book had me at "joy is a person"! Roland has captured one of the most important points, if not THE MAIN POINT, of being a Christian and turned it into a MUST READ... especially NOW, in these challenging times. He writes, "*joylessness is an epidemic, and a challenge we were created for—provoking and inviting us to contend for the pure and vibrant joy of God to be experienced and established in our own lives and in our world.*" Let's get our master's in the "theology of joy" through this book where Roland will teach us, impart to us, guide us, heal us and open our hearts that we may live in the joy of the Lord, "put our faces in the sunlight," and make it contagious.

SUZY YARAEI

Songwriter, poet, worship leader

Co-founder KS Ministry

The church is most often caricatured by grumpy, baptized-in-lemon-juice, anemic Christianity. Roland invites us to see a biblical worldview of joy in everyday life. Jesus' ministry was marked and overflowing with joy. It's what made Him attractive to kids and the outcast. It's also joy that sustained as He approached the pain of the cross. It was for the joy set before Him that He endured the cross.

Roland's insight into living from joy is both beautiful and fortifying. He weaves aspects of the nature of God that are available to be experienced by every believer. He helps us see what the Kingdom of God really looks like. C.S. Lewis said that "'joy is the serious business of heaven." This book is serious. It is equipping, and it unlocks the joy of the Lord in you. Read it. It will make you seriously joyful.

JULIAN ADAMS

Director of Frequentsee

Internationally recognized prophetic voice

Author of *Terra Nova: Your call to redeem the earth and make all things new*, *The Kiss of the Father* and *Gaining Heaven's Perspective*.

www.frequentsee.org

THE SURPRISING
POWER OF

Joy

**RECLAIMING THE FORGOTTEN FRUIT
OF THE SPIRIT TO RELEASE
HEAVEN'S ATMOSPHERE**

ROLAND WORTON

DESTINY IMAGE® PUBLISHERS, INC.

P.O. Box 310, Shippensburg, PA 17257-0310

"Promoting Inspired Lives."

This book and all other Destiny Image and Destiny Image Fiction books are available at Christian bookstores and distributors worldwide.

Cover design by Eileen Rockwell
Interior design by Terry Clifton

For more information on foreign distributors, call 717-532-3040.

Reach us on the Internet: www.destinyimage.com.

ISBN 13 TP: 978-0-7684-5370-6
ISBN 13 eBook: 978-0-7684-5371-3
ISBN 13 HC: 978-0-7684-5373-7
ISBN 13 LP: 978-0-7684-5372-0

For Worldwide Distribution, Printed in the U.S.A.
1 2 3 4 5 6 7 8 / 24 23 22 21 20

Dedication

This book is dedicated to John Paul Jackson (1950-2015) and Jean Darnall (1922-2019), two uniquely gifted leaders who significantly impacted my life and leadership development. Thank you for seeing from Heaven's vantage point and calling me into fullness. Your example remains an inspiration to me.

Acknowledgments

My remarkable wife, Shirin, you are an incredible woman, wife, and mother, and a gift to me in so many ways. Thank you for enabling me to write, for modeling the joy that I write about here, and for praying us into God's preferable future. To my two sons of thunder, I am incredibly proud to be your father—my prayer is that you apprehend the fascinating and un-depleted joy of God every day of your lives, and generously give it away to a generation that is hungry to meet the joyful Father.

To my incredible parents and immediate family, I am indebted to you for your consistent love and support.

To our closest friends near and far, thank you for bringing joy into our lives. We are richer because of your friendship.

To the Sojourn leaders and community, I am truly thankful for your pioneering spirit, consistent generosity, and mature expression of the Spirit-led life. It is a pleasure to lead as part of your pastoral team.

To the spiritual leaders who have personally equipped and strengthened us in various phases: Jean Darnall, Alan and LaDonna Elliot, Sam and Linaria Yeghnazar, Rod and Julie Anderson, Terry and Susan Moore, John Paul Jackson, and Bill and Susan Atwood. Your impact upon our lives is immeasurable.

To the various leaders and underground church networks in the Middle East, your lives lived in total dedication to Jesus have changed us, and your lived-out joy in the middle of persecution is contagious and humbling. You know who you are. We love you.

To the BLN community—thank you for being a place to land and belong.

To the various and wonderful friends and leaders who kindly agreed to write endorsements, thank you for lending your voice to this message and taking time out of your weighty schedules to stand with us.

Thank you to Destiny Image Publishers, for running with this message in this season—it is a pleasure to work alongside you.

Finally, to our Soundforgers Board and partners, thank you for investing into our global assignment and sound—you are helping us raise and impact a generation.

Contents

Introduction

*T*he God of joy, and therefore the joy of God, are permanently accessible to us through the "It is finished" of the cross, and the absolute victory of the resurrection of Jesus. Yet, joylessness in the Church and culture is an epidemic. Researching and writing this manuscript has coincided with one of the most personally challenging seasons of ministry that I have ever walked through for a variety of reasons. In addition, conceptualized over a year before publication, it is interesting that it is now being released during a global pandemic that has changed the face of culture like few things have in this generation. Anything and everything that we rely upon for entertainment, comfort, refreshing, and normality has been removed from us.

It is ironic then, most of all to me, that I am writing a book focused upon joy during a time in my life and culture, where in the natural joy has been quite difficult to find. God and I have talked extensively about this, and we have laughed. I have cried. Unrenewed parts of my thinking have wanted me to retreat from writing and resume again when joy was dripping from every crevice of my life. But the Father—the everlasting, uncaused, self-existent One, the self-sufficient, self-sustaining, luminous, radiant One—loves to choose the darkest but most opportune times to speak. If there was ever a time to rediscover and recapture the fullness of the joy of God in the Church and in our culture, it is now. I am aware that the content here represents only one dimension of what God may be speaking to us, and therefore do not claim to speak the final word on the subject of the Father's joy. Equally, it was not the primary intent to write a perfectly balanced book that would include every angle on the subject of joy found in Scripture. However, we are going to gather around and explore the subject of joy, unapologetically.

My hope is that you will be inspired to reclaim and rediscover joy on an unprecedented level, because we will need it for the days ahead. As you will discover, joy for followers of Jesus is not dependent upon or determined by our circumstances, whether challenging or full of ease. Joy instead is an inward marking, an inside furnishing provided by Holy Spirit that is available to us permanently, consistently, and without end. Never diminished in itself, as it comes from Him, and as we will learn, joy is found in Him as an attribute of Himself. Rather, our response to it, our awareness of it, or our ability to cooperate with joy can become tarnished for various reasons. If we let it.

This manuscript is to be a reminder that joy is who God wants to be for us; and more than that, a reminder that the Joy Giver lives *in us* and wants to operate dynamically *through us* to bring change to our spheres of influence. We are invited to cultivate the internal atmosphere of our lives so that it spills over, impacting and shaping the atmosphere that surrounds us, so others get to experience it. It is almost as if we were created to be God-carriers. Imagine that. A people through whom He would dwell in and manifest His presence through. Now that is a thought worth thinking.

It is an honor for me to imagine your life and journey being impacted as you read and expand in Him. My prayer is that profound measures, dimensions, and atmospheres of joy would emanate from your life so dynamically that earthquakes of joyful change would happen everywhere you walk—just as it did with Him.

1

Reclaiming Joy

*F*or centuries, the Church has gathered around the ancient creed that states, "Man's chief end is to glorify God, and to enjoy Him forever."[1] However, it is difficult at times to believe that God's people actually *enjoy* Him, or believe that God could actually enjoy Himself and others, simply because of the way we have often misrepresented Him and His ways of dealing with us. It is interesting that the apostle Paul describes the Kingdom of God as "righteousness, peace, and joy in the Holy Spirit" (Romans 14:17), listing *joy* unapologetically as one of three key attributes. If joy is mentioned as one-third of the Kingdom by a man who walked with Jesus and led and shaped the first-century Church while spending extended time in prison, it is probably wise for us to consider investing more time aligning with this dimension of the Kingdom.

To *reclaim something* not only implies that it has already been lost or stolen, but that it is also available to us and that we have a right to reclaim it. The Spirit of God is inviting us to *rediscover and reclaim joy on an unprecedented level*—both individually and as a culture. Jesus paid the ultimate price to grant us access to the Father's joy, to restore us to the Father, and inaugurate a Kingdom of joy that we would demonstrate just as He did. There is no lack of joy in the Father or in Heaven, so representing the God kind of joy to the world is part of what we *do*, and who we are to *be* as the Church lighting up the darkest places.

During times of immense intensity in a culture that seeks to discourage, defeat, and diminish our hope, there is actually a *greater invitation* for the Church to again embrace and practice joy on an unparalleled level—walking in a tangible reality of the joy that is found only in the Kingdom and in the Father Himself. For every challenge, God has already provided an answer and a provision to match it. Heaven *always* has the final word.

As believers in Jesus, by our very nature we are designed to live in a contrary reality to much of culture. Not in unreality or being unable to relate, but modeling a counterculture that speaks, responds, and acts from a heavenly perspective and from a heavenly supply. It is actually our privilege and a facet of our inheritance to model something that is otherworldly, a countercultural reality that comes from our Father's Kingdom, the King's domain.

When Jesus taught the disciples to pray "on earth as it is in heaven,"[2] He was revealing many things. One is that this realm—our reality—is to be transformed to reflect as much as possible the realm and reality of God. So, what is our response to having access to this Kingdom reality called joy? What if the measure of joy that the Church has previously been experiencing is only just scratching the surface of what is actually available to us? What if we have relegated joy to an emotion that may or may not surface when we experience positive things in life?

My conviction is that rediscovering the joy of the Father is going to be one of the most powerful and revolutionary adjustments that God is inviting us into, and one of the greatest weapons that the Church will carry in the season ahead. It will change atmospheres, break through heaviness, disarm and dismantle religious spirits, and ultimately strengthen us for the great and seemingly impossible exploits that we are designed for.

We often bypass key concepts about joy revealed in God's Word because we have stopped believing that joy is what He wants to be for us; or alternatively, certain truths in Scripture become clichés for us, instead of a heavenly reality that God intends for us daily.

> *Rejoice in the Lord always: and again I say, rejoice* (Philippians 4:4 KJV).
>
> *Rejoice always, pray continually, give thanks in all circumstances; for this is God's will for you in Christ Jesus* (1 Thessalonians 5:16-18 NIV).

These well-known and often overlooked verses have become freshly potent for me as I have studied and delved into the meaning of the word *rejoice*. Rejoicing in the Lord is a phrase that may sound outdated to us, maybe even out of touch. We would not necessarily run to use this terminology in our aim to stay relevant to culture! Maybe the Philippians 4:4 Scripture was written on a fridge magnet that you remember growing up, or part of a children's song that you sang. But there is formidable truth from the heart of God wrapped up in this one small sentence.

The word *rejoice* originates from a historic derivative of the French language, and actually means "to return to joy." The prefix *re* marks a return, similar to many other words in our current vocabulary: re-turn, re-discover, re-capture, re-fresh. The ending "joice" is a progenitor of the modern-day word *joy*. In reading this Scripture again, as "Return to joy in the Lord always, and again I say return to joy," carries so much more weight and life for us. The fact that it is *also a command* underlines the significance that God places on joy for us. It is not presented as a good suggestion, but as an imperative command; and just like all commands in Scripture, it contains within it the potential to fulfill itself as we obey. God never asks us to do something that He won't empower us to walk in. God's invitation into obedience contains within itself the inevitable promise of blessing.

Maybe like me, you are now looking at this Scripture a little different from before. I want to invite you to practice absorbing Scripture through this lens every time you read the word *rejoice* and experience a returning to the joy in your own life, which is always available in the Father.

Joy is a Person. Joy originated with God and is a default of God Himself—therefore, a reality of Heaven, and reflected in creation, as we will discover. The story of creation begins with the most beautiful garden[3]—a paradise that man was given to develop and enjoy, and ends with a feast, a marriage supper,[4] a gloriously extravagant, joyful, cosmic celebration. If you are not sure about enjoying yourself, then you probably need to prepare, because Heaven is going to be a celebration without comparison. Imagine a garden paradise and the most amazing feast for a moment.

These are the images, the "language" that God chose to speak when sharing the bookends of His creation process with us— Eden and Heaven. He is reminding us that we were made for places of beauty and joy, and that He loves to relate to us in terms of joyful realities. Jesus was the final bridge between Heaven's joy and earth's fall—His finished work through the cross and resurrection connecting us back to the unbroken intimacy of the Garden and securing our future place at the Feast of the Ages. The price of this restoration was the scandal of the cross, and the joy set before Him was us.[5] The Bridegroom was buying back the bride. It was the joy of having all of God's sons and daughters reconnected to their place in the Father that compelled Him. Scripture tells us that He will wipe every tear from our eyes,[6] and that there will be no more *death, mourning, crying or pain.* Joy is a reality in Heaven. There is *joy in Heaven.* Have we allowed the implication of this to really saturate us?

However, we are not simply called to relegate the joy of Heaven to a future age. Access is a key concept in the New Testament discourse. The reality that we have access to God *now,*[7] in a way that we did not before the cross, is a major theme in Scripture and a powerful truth and reality for us as children of God. We have access and can interface with Him through the presence of Holy Spirit who lives in us. As we will discover, this is a pivotal truth in us understanding, embracing, and walking in joy at new levels. We live in the overlap between our present reality and Heaven's.

Jesus would not have taught us to pray for the Kingdom to come on earth if the Father did not intend to answer. He would not have revealed to us that the Kingdom of righteousness, peace, and joy in the Holy Spirit *is resident within us*,[8] if He did not intend for us to steward and release it in this realm. We are created to interact, interface with, and rediscover God's intended joy *now*, for our own lives and the world around us. God is inviting us to rediscover a theology of joy in the middle of the most challenging circumstances. Out of His own supply and inclination, the Father, in advance, intended to furnish us with joy inside that would literally color everything we touch with the substance of His joy. We are joy carriers and dispensers by design.

I want to be clear that I don't believe God is obligated to make us "happy," but that He *has promised to provide us with joy*. For the purposes of our conversation here, it is important to differentiate between the two. Happiness can be defined as an emotion driven by, or dependent upon, the expectations of external circumstances being fulfilled; and it can come or go, hoping that we will be happy *when* this or that happens. Conversely, we are often not happy *because* something that we wanted did not manifest in the way that we expected.

Joy, however, dives a little deeper and is the fruit of the life of God working inside us as we align and cooperate with His will for our lives—loving what He loves and becoming more like Him. Joy for the Christian has its source in God, is everlasting, functions regardless of circumstances, and is not dependent upon mood or outcome. Joy is fuel from the resurrected Jesus, the joyful One, to walk in this world as His representation.

We love to quote it, "the joy of the Lord is your strength,"[9] but we are invited to actually live it. I am excited to journey with you in discovering new advantageous places of joy and all of its attributes *within you* that will be given away, distributed, and released *through you* as part of God's Kingdom invasion to the world *around you.*

WHAT HAS GOD BEEN RELEASING?

Before delving into various facets of joy, it is important to take a glimpse at the big picture that provides context for what God has been releasing in our generation. In looking at church history, we can identify different *eras of emphasis;* some are seismic shifts that shaped the emerging church for generations afterward such as the Reformation in the 16th century and the birth of the Pentecostal outpouring at the beginning of the 20th century. Other eras are smaller in scope, maybe affecting or birthing certain movements or church streams, but can nevertheless be recognized as the finger of God restoring or emphasizing dimensions of His Kingdom that He wants the Church to carry in a particular time in history.

During these surges, the universal foundational doctrines of Christianity do not change, the ones that were worked through and established in the first few centuries of the early church through various councils of leaders.[10] There are seasons however, when the Spirit of God clearly breathes life into certain emphases and themes that were not recently practiced, seen, or experienced, or maybe even lost to an entire segment or generation of the Body of Christ. It is important to identify these, and Scripture encourages us to "hear what the Spirit is saying to the churches."[11] These distinctives are like the fingerprints of God, or changes to the "sound" that the Church is both hearing and amplifying.

I want to suggest to you a number of these more recent restorations to the global Church. Others may choose to describe these using different vocabulary, and there may be some missing that others would feel are crucial. Some have been pioneered by a few early adopters for a long time, and now many others are engaged and even releasing new expressions of what others previously started. It is not my aim to provide a definitive list, but to gather around the context of what God is doing in our generation, and to provoke questions in you as what this means as we "do" church, and what we can discover about where the power of joy may fit in all of this.

Some observations:

- An emphasis upon the Kingdom of God as the context for the Church—the Church is not the Kingdom, the Church operates within the Kingdom.

- A celebration of a lifestyle of ongoing personal renewal, encounter with Holy Spirit, and the love of the Father.

- An expectation for the empowering of all believers to carry and release the Kingdom on earth as it is in Heaven.

- Widespread proliferation of worship and intercession through houses of prayer, 24/7 prayer, and strategic prayer initiatives.

- The expectation of signs, wonders, and miracles inside and outside the church. The facilitation of healing, healing rooms, healing evangelism.

- The acceptance of Holy Spirit-led inner healing or personal ministry models and the integration of them into the life of the local church.[12]

- Prophetic activation outside the four walls of the church—words of knowledge, user-friendly prophecy, and dream interpretation for evangelistic thrust and to influence marketplace and business initiatives.

- Increased awareness and function of apostolic, prophetic, pastoral, evangelistic, and teaching gifts and anointings both inside and outside the church to equip and advance the Kingdom.

- Transformation of culture through impacting spheres of influence and the activation of the Church to engage business and the marketplace.

- Increased engagement with social justice, practical serving of public services in cities and regions, and leaning into positively shifting measurable markers of transformation in cities and regions— poverty, crime, sex-trafficking, unemployment, education, domestic abuse, abortion rates, incarceration, etc.

- The emergence of the Church online through social media engagement, digital communication, and mobilization.

Along with these observable traits, we have been experiencing a philosophical shift in the way the Church functions and operates. Although there is nothing necessarily wrong with where we were, it is as though the Father is emphasizing truer-truths as the Church matures in this generation. We have been moving from:

- Church focus to Kingdom focus
- Individual focus to corporate focus—from me to we
- Gifts inside the church to transformation outside the church
- Exalting an emphasis to integrating multiple emphases
- Waiting for an open heaven to living under a permanent open heaven
- God works through me
- Meetings to mobilization
- Teaching to activation
- Release of the Spirit to the release of the Kingdom
- One-generational thinking to multigenerational purpose

In order to fulfill what God is asking us to do, we need a heightened level and intensity of joy. Some are afraid that we may emphasize joy and celebration too much at the detriment of doctrine or discipleship. Maturity should inform us that we do not need either/or but both/and. It is terrible that there are extremes of sadness, suicide, depression, and oppression in our world; but our God has released His extreme joy unreservedly not simply to counterbalance the darkness, but to transform it beyond recognition. It is true for the Christian that we are called to move beyond personal joy so that there is enough for us and enough to give away—enough to infuse the sphere of influence[13] we have been given. Way beyond an emotion or a feeling that we should allow to be sidelined, instead we are discovering that joy is intended as part of the Father's design for us.

In the next chapter we explore the incredible joy-filled nature of our Father and how we can make room for His joy in us in new ways. Before doing that, there some frameworks that are important to consider and will be helpful for us to reclaim the joy that He wants to give us.

SIGNIFICANT LENSES

In building a framework for us to reclaim, experience, and walk in increasing joy, several key concepts are useful for us to personally consider:

- Our capacity for joy.
- Our ability to receive.
- Our awareness of depletion.

It is easy to back away and leave the issue of joy entirely to God—shifting it into a category beyond our responsibility or ability—living as though there is simply nothing we can do about it. But mysteriously, God loves to invite us into partnership with Him. Inviting us into brokering dimensions of who He is into the world around us as His representatives, even when He clearly carries capacity to do most things quite well by Himself. In one sense, there is nothing we can do to earn more of Him; and yet equally, we get to choose to respond to an invitation to host more of Him and what He is doing. The issue is not that we won't *have* joy—because I believe it is an inbuilt deposit available to every believer—but the truer issue is *how much of it* we will have at our disposal? Enough just for us to survive, or enough to give away? How much joy capacity will we steward?

When we refer to *capacity,* we are talking about honestly assessing and evaluating our ability to house the joy that God wants to give us. The size of our joy container. Jesus talked in terms of "fullness" of joy,[14] so there must be a way of measuring joy and evaluating a sense of capacity. Is there room for joy in our lives? In *your* life? What would it look like to walk in *fullness* of joy? These may seem like a strange questions, but ones we should endeavor to answer.

It is interesting to me that Jesus sometimes asked the obviously sick if they wanted to get well.[15] He was never looking for an answer to something that He didn't already know, but inviting them into a process of self-perceiving what was in their *own* hearts. In asking what predominantly fills our lives, our time, our thoughts, our conversations, and our focus, we are taking inventory of causative aspects of our daily routine. Causative, because they are actions and decisions that *cause* certain outcomes and either add to or decrease the potential joy we experience. If we do not appreciate some of the results that we are currently experiencing in our lives, maybe we can consider making changes to root causes and the actions that stem from them? Is there capacity in our lives for joy, or are we filled to capacity with something else? How big is our overall capacity to host something that God wants to give us and pour through us?

Second, taking a look at our ability or willingness to *receive* is also an important factor. Experience tells us there is often a significant gap between what is offered to us and what we *actually* decide to receive. God can be generously and unceasingly pouring out, but we simply may not have positioned our hearts to adequately receive. This can be true for a number of reasons. For example, a Wi-Fi signal that is perfectly transmitting is not necessarily picked up by an iPad, just because it has Wi-Fi capacity. If we do not believe that joy is something that God wants to give us and actually makes available *for* us, we may not even know that we should open ourselves to receive it.

In so many areas of our God journey, we can simply live in far less than is available to us because of lack of knowledge. Along with this, we may not recognize our call to *steward joy* as a fruit of the Spirit. We easily make room for love, peace, and patience, and we cultivate kindness, faithfulness, gentleness, and self-control. But sometimes we leave joy aside as an anomaly, a random force that may or may not blow our way. As Christians, we often have a concept that God wants to give us joy, but may have not necessarily spent time cultivating a place for it in our lives. We can even unknowingly block joy, considering it as immature or not as *serious* as love. Or we simply don't see our need for it. Maybe we are gifted in other areas and have fullness there, and joy is simply a welcomed addition, but not a crucial necessity. We'll just be fine as we are. We will be joyful when we get to Heaven, I guess?

Saying yes to God and whatever He wants to give us, is part of a lifestyle of receiving. It positions us in humility that is attractive to Him. When we are aware that we have not accessed everything that has been made available to us, we are open to more. Realizing that everything has been made accessible, but we have not necessarily appropriated it. The paradox of life in the Kingdom is that we have been given fullness, yet the Apostle Paul clearly says he will *press on* toward the goal and take hold of what Christ did for him.[16]

We could say it this way, that cultivating a hunger and receptiveness to joy is not an issue of striving more but *aligning more* with what is already available to us. Switching on the ability to receive. Saying yes to the joy that He has for us. Holy Spirit is the most incredible connector and interface. He is the very Spirit of God and carries all of Heaven's storehouse with Him. The first step to receiving the Father's joy is receiving Holy Spirit. We get to ask what leaning into the Holy Spirit moment by moment looks like for us. Do we know how to do that? He is ready to teach us. Is there a sense of cooperating with Him in what we may think is the mundane and routine of life, so that we can partner with Him with something powerful when it shows up?

Take a moment right now. However close to Holy Spirit you have been in the past, or are now, there is always more to discover and delve into. He is the ultimate Friend. Spend a few moments talking with Him, letting Him know from your own heart the greater intimacy and connection that you would like to have. Respond to the invitation that is always there, permanent, and 24/7.

We can continue when you pick back up.

• • •

It is always powerful to take a moment to reconnect with the Holy Spirit. He never leaves us, but during the busyness of life we can sometimes disconnect from awareness of what He is doing, saying, and being. There is always fruitfulness in greater connectivity with Him.

Finally, awareness of a decrease or attempted *depletion* or diversion of joy helps us retain God's intended joy in our daily walk. With increased capacity for joy, and openness to receive, we will naturally begin to experience dimensions of Father's joy move through our lives. The extent and depth to which we host this as a permanent resource for our own lives and for others, is dependent on various factors. One of which is the extent to which we recognize and stop the redirection of joy *out* of our lives.

The concept of *siphoning* is useful here. This is a word that is not used often now but describes the deliberate and intentional draining of a resource—the gradual, often secretive stealing and depletion of a necessary reserve. Responsibilities, callings, distractions, people, needs—both positive and negative—can actually become the very things that deplete the reserves of joy in our lives. Areas that are supposed to be experiencing the burst and benefits of joy coming through us are actually slowly depleting our reserves, causing us to run dry. The good news is that Holy Spirit is the Master Hydrator and will show us how to prevent the diversion and siphoning of God's amazing resources in our lives.

What do we need to reclaim in order to reverse the process of depletion? Staying connected to God and fresh each day is crucial—gathering life, hope, peace, and wisdom for all that we are involved with, and also watching for the subtle or not so subtle diversion of power and joy from our lives. If our joy reserve is completely focused and used up on one area alone, it cannot be available to be used somewhere else.

The Father absolutely wants to surprise us with the power of His joy in new and undiscovered dimensions. Literally destroying the false perceptions of what joy should look like in our lives, and even the limits and restrictions we have placed on it. I believe that it is the Father's heart that we rediscover fresh joy as the Body of Christ. There are deposits of Heaven's joy that are here to match whatever comes in our generation, and we are invited to lean into and cooperate with His Kingdom and His presence, making room and responding to the invitation to journey with Him and *become* everything He intends for us to become. This requires us to position ourselves and lean in—responding in order to have the greatest capacity for joy that God intends for us, increasing in our ability to receive it, and closing pathways that cause it to be diverted or depleted in our lives. This is our part of the partnership. His commitment is to supply joy without cost, and without limits.

And so the real question is, are you ready to experience more of the Father's joy in your life?

As we begin to make room for Holy Spirit to create an increased capacity and expectancy for joy, the following concepts are really useful to consider, and will reappear throughout the book in various forms:

- Thinking redemptively
- Transformational perspective
- Expecting and anticipating upgrades

These concepts can be likened to lenses that we look through. Each one is important as God leads us in the cultivation of fresh joy in our lives.

THINKING REDEMPTIVELY

The theme of *redemption* is prominent in Scripture and is seen most clearly through Jesus purchasing us with His own blood, resulting in us being redeemed by Him and for Him. In this very real sense, we are already redeemed if we are "in" Christ. In addition to this, we can also think in terms of *redemptive gifts*, which are the God-given, hard-wired giftings in individuals, regions, or people groups that are redeemed or activated in relationship with God through alignment to Him and His ways. In this way, we understand that individuals, people groups, and even nations carry unique expressions, gift-mixes, and attributes found in God Himself. These redemptive gifts permeate their function and identity and influence their particular contribution to the world. Some of these gifts that God intends remain unredeemed and are used for the advancement of darkness—others are redeemed and used to advance God's Kingdom depending on who we serve and whose we are.

Thinking redemptively causes us to *relate to people and things in their redeemed identity*, whether they have submitted to the ways and will of God or not. Thinking redemptively grants us the privilege of relating to people and things *according to God-given potential*, not current performance. The invitation is to make ourselves available to see God's redemptive purpose and power in every person and circumstance that we encounter. We get to step into adventures with God that bring change and life as we *remind people who they are really meant to be*, seeing joy increase as we step out and see Him move.

Our default becomes, "God, I know that You are always working toward redemptive outcomes. What are *You* doing in this situation?" and, "What do You want *me* to do in this situation?" In relationship, we get to pause for a moment and dialogue with Him about what He is doing, and what our role is.

Sometimes we can step out in assumption and then demand that God back us up in what we would like to see happen. Alternatively, we can look to Jesus and what He modeled for us. There was tremendous power and authority in Jesus' ministry because He *only* did what He saw His Father doing, and *only said* what He heard His Father say. Of course, the great mandates of Scripture[17] tell us our job description, so we do not have to guess what He has already sent us to do. However, timing, application, specific ways God wants to move, and our role in the moment becomes clarified when we simply ask.

Thinking redemptively is giving ourselves permission to *look at life and individuals through a grid of hope, from the Father's perspective.* Jesus modeled this for us in many ways, as we will explore later. Choosing to look for and discover the redemptive purpose of God built into every person and circumstance is part of our design. A practice, a choice, a lifestyle of joy cultivation.

TRANSFORMATIONAL PERSPECTIVE

Some of the greatest joys in God's story surround the consistent issue of transformation. We do not have abundant space to focus on this here in a book dedicated to exploring joy. However, there are realities that are important as we push into the fight for our own joy, and the joy of those around us. Scripture is abounding in examples of circumstances, peoples, lands, futures, cities, systems, and family lines that were caught between a *seemingly barren reality and a future hope* needing transformation.

To transform means to change the form of; a change of shape; to experience metamorphosis; to move beyond (*trans*), the current form. There is not often an abundance of joy attached to the pre-transformation places. They are hard and depleting, "not conformed to the image of God" places. Maybe dark, and definitely not emanating joy. So, we get to show up with His abundant joy. How will we or the world wonder at His wonders if there are no evidences of His wonderfulness demonstrated to places that are impossible? The children of God are the one's equipped to see a preferable future, a prophetic picture of what something can look like touched by our transforming God. Just one encounter with Him and people experience metamorphosis and transformation. They move beyond their current form and further into the image of Jesus.

Abram was transformed into Abraham, the father of nations. Jacob the deceiver was transformed into Israel, the namesake of the people of promise. Noah's wooden boat was transformed into a new beginning for God's creation. A fearful, unprepared group of followers were transformed into apostles of the early church who turned the world upside down;[18] and the journey of Jesus from death to His resurrection was the greatest transformational moment in all of history.

Allowing yourself to live with a mindset of transformational possibility is a key to hope and a key to joy.

The well-known passage from Romans 8:28 offers a promise to us: "that all things work together for good to those who love

God, to those who are called according to His purpose." This is an invitation from God to align and make room for the reality of this truth to be manifest. This is the crux of transformational possibility. There will always be something that we need to trust God for. What is interesting to me is that this verse is followed directly by the truth that we are being "conformed to the image of His Son," Jesus. He is making us more like Him in our journey.

Heaven is absolutely committed to us being *transformed* into the image of Christ. Embracing the "all things work together for good" and the being "conformed to the image" of Jesus is not always a combination that we like to buy into. We usually want to lean into one or the other, nonchalantly brushing off reality because it will all just work out, or conversely gritting our teeth through a forced smile because we believe that God consistently punishes us until we are force-conformed to be like Him. However, there is a glorious paradox to discover here that produces a beautiful and lasting joy. All things *are* working together for good; and alongside the process, there is an invitation into a shaping and conforming happening that causes me and you to emerge into a clearer image of Jesus, into the fullness of what we were created for, that we will take with us into eternity. This is wonderful to me, and so much richer.

There is an abundance of scriptural accounts where our God turns bareness into something wonderfully fruitful. Beauty for ashes.[19] God speaks metaphorically. It is part of His language. Get comfortable with God speaking metaphorically, because He does it a lot, and doesn't always ask our permission to do so. One of the foundations of the Father's Kingdom is transformation. Everything He does takes something that is untransformed, and under the banner of redemption moves it into something that is transformed through His love, power, purpose, redefinition, hope, and joy.

ANTICIPATING UPGRADES

God's intent is often manifested in the form of an upgrade. An exchange. Usually our deficiency in some area, for His sufficiency. Things that we cannot possibly earn. That which we are not capable to do on our own, He moves from kindness to restore to us to His original intent. This is true of salvation. He draws us, reveals Himself to us; and as we respond, He regenerates us, new creation happens, and we begin to manifest His characteristics, desires, and fruit through His Spirit now in us, in accordance with this new nature. This is all His work. It's astounding. Before we are born again, there is often an innate desire in us to *want to love,* but we often find ourselves defeated, because we are restricted in drawing from our own capacity to love, which outside of Jesus is often not enough for ourselves, let alone to give away.

When the love of the Father saturated me and broke into my own life, I was undone and made whole at the same time, and it impacted me in such a way that I have never been the same. I received an upgrade of love that was unlike anything imaginable. His wholeness supplanted my brokenness, uprooted rejection, and filled my reserves with love so fully that I was able to give away authentic love for the first time. True, other-centeredness was possible because I had experienced the other-centeredness of God Himself. Encountering the fullness of the indescribable love of God, we realize that there is more than enough for us, and more than enough to give away. This is the great exchange. This is the great upgrade.

A mindset that expects upgrades is the beginning place for individuals and a culture that desire to carry unreasonable faith and expectation. The Word of God, the Bible, reveals that He wants to give us the oil of joy for mourning and a garment of praise for a spirit of despair.[20] These are powerful upgrades. This was part of Jesus' ministry. Part of what He revealed of the Father to the world. He was pointing us to what the Father is like. He's the Father who exchanges what we don't have, for what He does. It's incredible. Righteousness for our filth. Love for fear.

> *For His anger is but for a moment, His favor is for life; weeping may endure for a night, but joy comes in the morning* (Psalm 30:5).

We like to lean into the second half of this verse that encourages us that weeping won't last long, and that joy is coming. This is a great thought. But there is an exchange and an upgrade here that is so much greater than that. The psalmist is actually comparing joy to a *lifetime* of favor and weeping to a *moment* of anger. For all of us, weeping is a reality. There are different kinds of weeping, and He has answers for all of them. For our purposes here, we don't have time to enter into the theological implications of lamenting and weeping, and the numerous and difficult situations that cause hurt and sadness to us and also to the heart of God. But I do know that He is passionately resolved against anything and everything that steals, kills, and destroys life, or distorts and impacts our intended design and relationship with Him.

I am certain that the wrath of God was poured out upon Christ through His sacrifice, and the punishment that bought us peace was laid upon Him.[21] In the grand scheme of things, the weeping of our days of rebellion and disconnect are like one night in the light of an eternity of relationship with Him. Joy comes unexpectedly like a new day in the middle of our maturing-trials, because a greater joy has already spoken. With joyful intent the Father exchanged the void and chaos for light[22] at the point of creation, and the angels sang for joy. The Son's arrival was announced with joy and a promise of favor for all humankind.[23] But ultimately, the greatest joy and the greatest upgrade—the "It is finished"—has been echoing throughout the universe since Jesus exchanged His blood for our depravity, defeating sin, sickness, death, and hell. This joy speaks today and speaks loudest. We must make room for it to resound in our souls, our lives, our communities, and our nations.

My prayer is that you will embrace redemptive thinking, transformational perspective, and an expectation for upgrades as you embark upon the journey to reclaim His fullness of joy in your life. To help you, at the end of each chapter, you will find steps to rediscovering and returning to joy. Please take a moment to engage in these before reading on. My hope is that these simple prompts will help personalize and clarify things for you, while also accelerating your joy journey.

• • •

REDISCOVERING JOY: STEP I

Engage in Prayer

> *Stop for a moment and engage with a Holy Spirit-inspired prayer. From your heart, ask Him for courage and revelation to begin to reclaim and rediscover His joy that is available to you in the Kingdom. Agree with God for a stepping into redemptive thinking, transformational hope, and an expectation for upgrades, and that all blockages to His intended fullness would be removed. He loves to answer our heartfelt prayer and He is waiting to move extravagantly on our behalf when we step out and ask.*

Reflection

- Take time to reflect upon how you may have let go of or retreated from joy in certain areas of your life. What is God saying to you about reclaiming joy, and what might that look like?

- Take time to think about your current capacity to return to joy when facing what life brings. Be honest. Are there any particular areas where it is difficult to find joy?

- Do you have a habit of looking at life through a joy-filled lens? Where can you shift your thinking to make more room for redemptive thinking, transformational hope, and expectation for upgrades from God?

Activation

- Plan to have a conversation with someone close to you, someone you trust. Ask the person their perception of your current joy level and to give you an honest assessment.

- There may be significant reasons why joy has been stolen from you, and all of the circumstances surrounding these issues may not yet be resolved. Making a decision that God's joy is available to you regardless and drawing a boundary around the future stealing of your joy are powerful steps you can take today.

- Begin to pray daily for a fresh release of joy from the Holy Spirit.

2

Joyful God

*I*t is an amazing moment when we grasp that we are made in God's image; and not only that, but *all* that is seen, everything created, was made out of who He is. God's Word literally tells us that "all that is visible was made out of what is invisible."[1] His realm is more real, than the realm that *we* call reality.[2] Joy then, is present in our world as an emotion, an experience, a fruit of the Spirit, a pervading atmosphere—simply because it is an attribute of God Himself.

By default, as the Originator of joy, our Father is the most joyful being who has ever or will ever exist. We see evidence of it through the beautiful, powerful, and contagious joy that we often experience as human beings at various times and in various ways. This mysterious thing called joy, along with everything else He has created, comes from Him and through Him. I cannot entertain any portrayal of God that does not make room for His joy in His dealings with us.

I absolutely embrace suffering, which we will discuss later, but the very nature of our adversary, who is the antithesis to everything that our Father is, makes it his purpose to release the opposite of joy into our world. Our enemy is the joy stealer, the destroyer of life, a thief that attempts to rob us of the very characteristics of the Father that we are called to carry and release to the world. Stated simply, joy is an attribute of God, and an attribute found in those who are called to be like Him.

> *Where were you when I laid the earth's foundation? Tell me, if you understand. Who marked off its dimensions? Surely you know! Who stretched a measuring line across it? On what were its footings set, or who laid its cornerstone—while the morning stars sang together and all the angels shouted for joy?* (Job 38:4-7 NIV)

In the middle of a discussion with Job, who was walking through the middle of an intense, transformative season, God invites him into an enlarged vision of who He is, and who He wants to be for Job. By the end of the story, God abundantly restores everything that was lost, and everything that was stolen. But at this moment, God is reminding Job that he can trust in His big-ness because He was there at the very beginning and even before the very beginning, as Creator.

What is fascinating to me is the picture that is painted in the Scripture passage. Morning stars sang, and angels *shouted for joy*. This moves me. As the Creator worked and spoke "let there be light" into the void, into the chaos where there was nothing—something He still loves to do today—the morning stars sang in response, and the angels shouted. They shouted for joy. Envision thousands of angelic beings roaring with joy as the plans for creation begin to unfold.

All worship is a response to who He is. This shout for joy from the angels was a response to the revealing of God's greatness and glory. In my previous book, *Emerging Worship*, I lay out a mandate for the reclamation of powerful worship in our generation—releasing our own unique sound, but also becoming a voice for Heaven's sound to invade earth. Joining with angels, we too are called to shout for joy in response to who He is.

I love hearing shouts of joy. There are some people in my life who just have it in regard to shouting for joy. They do it a lot. Whether in response to something astounding, something funny, or just because they are pleased to see me. Every time I hear a genuine shout for joy, it reminds me of something that I want to rediscover. As a father, there was nothing greater than hearing my children release joy-shouts when they were small. We experience waves of cheering and explosions of joy from sports fans in stadiums all around the world. It's expected. Just hearing it, invites us into the experience. It's my observation that the church in many instances has reversed out of this place of shouting for joy. Maybe it's not comfortable? Or we believe that it is irreverent. Or we believe we are called to be *only* serious.

There is a lie regarding shouting and God. Let me tell you what it is. It takes on various disguises, but basically implies that God is offended at joy and noise, that quietness is more reverent; and therefore by default, shouts of joy must be irreverent. This infers that God cannot handle the emotions that He created us with. When combined with the sense of overwhelming shame that many can live in, not knowing what He's really done for us and who we really are in Christ, we have a perfect storm. In an environment that says, I am not acceptable to God, and He is also offended at any raw expression of emotion that I can offer to Him, the lid is firmly on.

The people of God become locked in a double bind. What do I mean by this? If a problem that I am facing originates with me, then God can break me through somehow as I walk with Him. But if I also believe there is a fundamentally immovable problem on God's end such as He's offended at joy, then it is going to be impossible to ever believe that there is a way out, or that opportunity for change exists. This concept can create problems in our perception regarding healing, destiny, and decisions along with many others. We can "set God free" from what we have projected onto Him by giving ourselves and His Church permission to fully engage being ferociously in love with God, with all of its emotion and volume. Of course, we do not live by our feelings, and there are moments to be awestruck silent in His presence, and Scripture talks about this. But not because we believe that it will please God more than being loud. This is simply not true.

It is so important to know that joy is a very attribute of God, and because it's an attribute of God, it flows into the created order; it was there at the beginning of creation, and it is *present today*. The angelic beings that witnessed the Father creating, shouted for joy in response. I'm going to go as far as saying that because He created *in* joy and *from* joy, the very act of creation is joy-causative; it has the potential to create a response of joy in those who see and witness it.

Everything that He does is good and perfect, and His constant transformative work in our lives and the lives of others ignites a response. The God of Joy does wonderful things; and when we see and experience them, we become joyful too. If, that is, we allow ourselves to go there. The utter complexity, wonder, irrefutable intelligence, and supernatural activity involved in so many attributes of creation are joy-filled moments waiting to happen. We have all experienced this.

I was expecting the Grand Canyon to be inspiring the first time I saw it. I literally walked up the footpath to the rim with anticipation knowing that I would be impressed. But what happened to me physically was beyond being intellectually astounded. As I walked up to the edge and caught a glimpse of the vastness and magnificence, my mouth literally fell open. By itself. This had never happened to me before. And then I laughed. A wonder-filled, "Oh my goodness, no way," kind of laugh. You may be smiling as you read this because you have experienced this too. I was filled with an unusual joy as a response to Father's handiwork.

I like to think that God enjoys these moments, and that it was part of His intention when He was just being Himself in creating all of the incredible, awe-inspiring things in our world. I understand that everyday life is not filled with trips to the Grand Canyon, and it's sometimes challenging to search for joy in the somewhat mundane and seemingly unremarkable places of our daily routine. But what if we upgraded our thinking and lived from the reality that, if joy is an attribute of my Father's nature, then I'm going to look for Him and find joy whenever I can? What if we lived with a twenty-four hour radar that scanned and looked for His joy all the time? It would change us. It would change our world.

I want to be clear that I am not talking about positive thinking or mind over matter. I am simply inviting us into an understanding of joy as an attribute of God and something that He just *is*—along with healing, hope, and the peace that He releases. He heals because He *is life itself*—life flows so gloriously through Him that it restores and heals everything that it touches. Joy, hope, strength, peace, all work in the same way.

Maybe you have been walking through a season that has been particularly difficult and dark, and joy has not been easy to locate or take hold of. I personally understand those times. These are only seasons, though, that are not meant to be permanent. Remember, we walk *through* the valley of the shadow of death.[3] These parts of our journey don't get to define our nature, our future, or the level of joy we will walk in. Maybe you can take a moment now to put this book down and rediscover the Father as the God of Joy. Leaning into the truth that joy is found in Him, it is inseparable from Him, and it exists around Him and is found in His presence. The next paragraph will still be here when you continue. Take a moment.

• • •

I hope that as you took time to stop for a moment, to reflect on, breathe in, and allow yourself to be impacted by the Father of Joy, that you encountered Him in a new and powerful way. It's amazing to think that He will never exhaust His supply of love or joy. He is the incredible self-existent One and is never depleted. Not only is joy something that God is, but something that He gives away. The mystery of the Trinity reveals the God who is *other-centered*. Even in the interaction of the Godhead, we see relationship and community. God can be nothing else but giving. We see this in the way He has indelibly marked creation, but we also see this toward us.

As we talk about Him in these ways, can you feel fresh joy rising in you? I can. You have permission to enjoy God because it's His desire for you.

> *Thou hast made known to me the ways of life; thou shalt make me full of joy with thy countenance* (Acts 2:28 KJV).
>
> *You have made known to me the ways of life; You will enrapture me [diffusing my soul with joy] with and in Your presence* (Acts 2:28 AMPC).

These two different translations of Acts 2:28 quote King David and summarize who he knew God to be—the One who makes known to us paths of life, and whose countenance when turned toward us causes us to be full of joy, diffusing us with it in His presence. When we find Him and His ways, joy is right there.

As those who belong to the God of joyful intent, we might ask who He wants to be for us in the next season. What aspects of joy does He want to reveal and give to us as we begin to journey in reclaiming and rediscovering Him as our Father of Joy? We started deliberately with God, with the Foundation of all joy, and from there we ask who He wants to be for us in joy in the days ahead. When we exhibit attributes of authentic joy as His children, we are simply being more like our Father. What if Christ-likeness could be measured not only in church-centric activities, which are all important and valid, but also in new expressions of undiscovered joy that are found inherent in the Father, and who He is and wants to be through us in this world?

THE SINGING GOD

The LORD your God is with you, the Mighty Warrior who saves. He will take great delight in you; in his love he will no longer rebuke you but will rejoice over you with singing (Zephaniah 3:17 NIV).

The LORD thy God in the midst of thee is mighty; he will save, he will rejoice over thee with joy; he will rest in his love, he will joy over thee with singing (Zephaniah 3:17 KJV).

Zephaniah, a friend of God and a prophet, walked in the revelation that God sings. But not only sings. He *rejoices over us* when He sings. This is beautiful—that God Himself returns to joy over us. I believe that the Father wants to rewire the way we have perceived joy and the way we have aligned with it. When the God of creation rejoices over you—the One who says the nations are like drops of water[4] to Him, and who released the "Let there be light"[5] so that the sound of His voice is still expanding the galaxies even now—something has to shift. We were designed to *hear and receive* the joy that is inherently part of who God is. The Father is singing acceptance, delight, and joy, over you. Today. Personally.

As a young father, singing over my sons when they were tiny men was part of my routine to settle them, to familiarize them with the presence of God before they slept, and to speak destiny over them. The Father does the same for us. The song of God over us is not always comforting, but at times a rousing, raucous, "I'm proud of you" song. Another translation of Zephaniah 3:17 says He rejoices over us with "loud singing"!

When Jesus began His ministry and the Father announced Him to the world, saying, "This is My beloved Son in whom I'm well pleased," we may have tempered this moment in our imagination, reducing it to a reserved sacred statement. But just like the angels announced "great joy" when He was born, the Father announced His love and great pleasure over Jesus as He began His assignment. He was the One who's assignment had been planned before the foundation of the earth.[6] The eternal Son who was about to reveal the Father to all humankind, to defeat sin and death, and to seal the promise through rising from the dead!

I think that the Father was ecstatic and excited as He announced His pleasure over Jesus. This is *your* Father too. He is rejoicing over you with singing. As Zephaniah realized when joy was sung over him, He is *with* you too and mighty to save. This truth causes joy to rise in us. Experiencing His song over us is part of our inheritance. He loves to surprise us with the power of His joy.

What if an answer to some of the courage we need is not in pulling ourselves up in an attempt to be braver, but leaning into hearing His song over us? Until it becomes solidified in us that He is *with* us, and we can stand against any force of darkness in the One who is mighty to save. He is repositioning us so that we do not just understand *intellectually*, but actually live in the daily reality of His more-than-enough, overcoming joy. Part of the abundant life that Jesus promised us is living moment by moment in the reality that God is always more than enough—not simply in what He can *do* for us, or what He can *give* us, but through who He actually is. God *as* Himself, just *being* Himself.

THE GOD OF DELIGHT

It is so easy for us to skip over the concept of *delight* in Scripture. The translation of the Zephaniah passage uses the word *delight* to describe God returning to joy over us. Too many words and concepts in Scripture can easily become cliché for us. Throughout the Bible, we see numerous occasions of the delight of God over significant people, places, events, and circumstances. Where individuals are brought out of who they were and into who they are in the light of the Father's love, forgiveness, and pleasure. Amazing encounters. But what about now?

"God delights in me." Try saying it out loud. Try shouting it.

If we spend some time meditating on this and allowing it to impact us, it is incredibly profound. It might *even* change us. From Latin and French roots, the word *de-light* with the prefix *de* means of or from.[7] The word *delight* or "of-light" has connotations of illumination on behalf of both those delighting, and the recipients of the delight. Everything is better with light. The familiar analogy that shadows and darkness simply exist because of the absence of light is significant here. When God greatly delights in us and returns to joy while singing over us, what amazing hope potential this brings onto our horizon. It lights up every shadow. Zephaniah must have personally experienced the joy-song of God or had been with someone who had, and the Holy Spirit was revealing this reality to all of the generations to come.

So, let's try it again. "God delights in me." Louder this time.

We have a Father who delights greatly in us, who perceives us "in light" and who loves to sing over us. Our God, who is Light, truly sees us, our true nature, all that He created us to be without the residue of the Fall and separation from Him—*in* light and *of* light. Another way of saying He delights in us is that He illuminates greatly over us. Most people have experienced a picture of this: when someone we love really sees and affirms us in ways that we hadn't formulated words for yet, or even knew we needed. They are saying "I see you," recognizing who we are, and all that we are carrying. This de-light shines into what we may see dimly or only partly about ourselves. It works with giftings, talents, characteristics, aptitudes. In this atmosphere, unique fingerprints of who we are designed to be in this world and clues to the unique assignments that God has prepared for us are revealed.[8]

Earthly affirmation is wonderful, but what we are truly designed for is the illumination of the Father when He "delights greatly" in us, speaking revealed identity to us. Singing. Over. Us.

One more time. "God delights in me."

Living in the awareness that God sings may be a new concept for some believers. Maybe we are more comfortable with an academic perspective that Scripture is simply painting word pictures and metaphors. Or that the sounds we experience through creation, like the wind in the trees, represent God singing *symbolically*. Maybe listening for God's song over you sounds too incredibly fantastical for you to digest. Too unrealistic, impractical, unanchored. I understand. I believe in scientific order, academic methodology, administrative structure, and personal discipline. It actually takes a lot of it to write the book you're reading. So, please don't hear what I'm *not* saying.

But sometimes explaining away the supernatural takes more intellectual acrobatics than simply believing what Scripture reveals. I am personally convinced that the God who sent His only Son—who had lived eternally with Him as part of the relational Trinity for eternity past—into our earthly dimension, fully God and fully man, flesh incarnate, can sing over us if He wants to. It is quite easy for me to make the leap from knowing Him as the God who created the oceanic tide cycle in conjunction with the moon, and the infinitesimal subatomic quarks found in human cells to the God who also sings over us. The presence and beauty of music, melody, and sound in our everyday lives, and in our world is incredible to me. Music was present in God from the beginning, or we wouldn't experience it now. Selah.

It's time to receive the song of God over our lives. What if we woke every morning to the thought that God not only likes us, but delights greatly in us and is rejoicing, returning to joy over us? What if His song of acceptance, forgiveness, sonship, adoption, favor, and peace was powerful enough to return us to joy? The song of the "It is finished." It is imperative in the middle of the intensity that each generation experiences, that followers of Jesus recapture the revelation and the reality of God's delight for us—reclaiming the often forgotten fruit of joy that is part of our inheritance and identity as those who are to *look like Him* in this world.

We are often guilty of becoming highly driven, bogged down, shut down, burdened, stressed, angry, and discontent with many extremely crucial and vital issues that we contend with on a personal, citywide, and national level. This only *strengthens the necessity to make more room for the song of God* in our noise-filled, restless, unsettled, worried, often weary world. There are also portions of the Church that are so focused on God's wrath, anger, and rebuke that there is no room for the answers that His death and resurrection have already yielded, and the joy that He emanates by just being Himself. When the Church stops believing in and receiving the joy-song of God, where are those who don't know Him yet supposed to go?

Often, a delving into our own hearts with Holy Spirit reveals things that the Father's love wants to unburden us from—not only stress, mistrust, anxiety, worry, anger, and frustration but also the unsanctified mercy we have extended, the sense of justice that is driven by our own unhealed hurt and judgment, and our self-appointed ownership of burdens we can do both nothing about and have no sphere of influence to change. It is without a doubt that we are created to live for causes that are bigger than ourselves and to burn for passions that bring the unedited power of the Kingdom of God to affect catalytic change. But Jesus is not asking us to do any of this outside of the joy and peace that He provides.

It seems too simple to allow ourselves to just let go and live in the de-light of God, becoming those who when asked, point a finger up to Him, the singing joyful God who has already moved on our behalf, and whisper, "He delights in you." But the Good News is just that simple, and delightful. It just might make *us* want to sing too.

LAVISH LOVE

Forever would never be long enough to come to the end of an endless love.

–DAVID AND MELISSA HELSER

See what great of love the Father has lavished on us, that we should be called children of God! And that is what we are! (1 John 3:1 NIV)

The Church has been impacted by a fresh revelation of the love of the Father in an expanded way over the past few decades. Of course the truth is, this is not something new; it has been restored to the global Church in various ways in various eras in its 2,000-year history. Although the Charismatic movement, and subsequent renewal movements, are primarily focused on the activity of the Holy Spirit and the activation of the gifts of the Spirit, a significant component of what was and is being released into people's lives is increased intimacy with the Father, and a deeper revelation of His love.

The lavish love of God has been described in a thousand ways, with a million metaphors, and will continue to be. How can we ever come to the end of living astounded by a never-ending love? Many profound lovers of God have written, spoken, sung about, and demonstrated the vast and immeasurable love of God in multifaceted ways, and I am not going to attempt to add significantly to the narrative here. However, in a discussion about *lavish joy*, we cannot avoid talking about *lavish love*. Love and joy are inescapably linked.

The love of God is the foundation upon which everything else in our lives stands. Lavish and extravagant encounters with the love of God is what we are made for. We are changed by love; and the perfect love of our perfect Father naturally creates joy in us. We are loved, and because of this are joy-filled. The very nature of a love that has moved and still moves toward us creates a foundation, an atmosphere, an unmatched acceptance out of which joy simply and naturally flourishes. God's love is like a biosphere with a perfect environment, in which joy is not only sustained but multiplied.

Unconditional love, by default, releases joy. Unconditional love is the term we have coined to attempt to describe the vastness of a love that is literally indescribable. The description of love in First Corinthians 13 endeavors to tell us what God's love is like: patient, not proud, keeping no record of wrongs, always protecting, always hoping. Numerous parables in the Old and New Testaments share symbolic and beautiful analogies to help us grasp it.[9] We were made to thrive in the soil of unconditional love, and Father God is the only One who can love us unconditionally.

As you know, we often look for endless ways to secure this unconditional acceptance, sometimes allowing ourselves to manipulate or be manipulated, maintaining slavery to gods that destroy us. Anything at all to maintain a sense of acceptance. God offers us unconditional and uncontested love without strings attached and without slavery. You have heard it said a thousand different ways, but there is nothing we can do to make God love us more, and nothing we will do to make Him love us less. His love is so good that we have difficulty wrapping our minds and hearts around it. This is where Holy Spirit comes in, making God's love real, tangible, and present so that our spirit cries out, "Abba," because we know beyond doubt that we belong to Him as children of God.[10]

The list of the fruit of the Spirit in Galatians chapter 5 is wonderful for many reasons. It is a description of what life looks like when led, empowered, and motivated by the Father. Love, joy, peace, patience, kindness, goodness, faithfulness, gentleness, and self-control is what Holy Spirit carries and we get to host. In one sense these characteristics can only be present in our lives once we have experienced them for ourselves. When we have been encountered by true kindness, patience, and gentleness, we can then begin to be truly kind, patient, and gentle. Again, it all originates with Him. It is interesting to me that the first two fruit of the Spirit are love followed by joy.

It was the love of God that captured me when I first began to discover Him. I did not personally come into relationship with Jesus through fear. I was so broken and already living in my own personal hell—the opposite of the fruit of the Spirit—so, His goodness, tenderness, and love was simply irresistible to me. Today when I read that He is patient and kind, it resonates with me because this is how I first experienced Him. Through this love relationship and an insatiable appetite for His Word, and a desire to be with people who loved Him too, I learned what my new identity as a son meant for me. I discovered how new royalty had the privilege of living, acting, and responding; and so my attitudes, appetites, and behavior were transformed. The fruit of orphan living diminished and I began exhibiting the fruit of the Spirit, especially love and joy.

The purifying fire of holiness also visited later, where I realized the ramifications of living outside of His ways and will, and the pain, damage, loss, and destruction that sin causes. The love of the Father does not want anyone He created to suffer depletion or distortion of the full expression of who He made them to be. Love calls us to Himself and away from sin, not in attempt to keep anything good from us, but to provide a pleasant pathway to the best of blessing, fullness of purpose, and ultimate joy.

Giving and receiving love is one of the foundational elements of existence. Darkness fights this with everything because it knows that God *is* love, and that love never fails.[11] We will talk more about the things that come to block or distort our joy in a later chapter. Both giving and receiving love is so important, because among other things it causes a catalytic release of joy. We could almost say that love and joy were designed to be contagious. Just as intimacy within marriage is intended to be so fulfilling that it becomes one of the deepest wells of human fulfillment that we drink from. Likewise, receiving His love and then giving it away is part of our foundational design, unlocking the greatest places of joy and the greatest sense of purpose in us. God operates as a Giver, and we become the best version of ourselves when we do too.

Jesus Himself was the greatest living parable—Love Himself revealing the Father. The religious were not too happy with Him. He invaded a culture of rules and regulations that had become separated from the heart of God, where people were seeking to *earn* relationship with the Father. Jesus detonated the greatest explosions underneath their paradigms and mindsets. Not just intellectually speaking, but in real time, in reality, in ways that dramatically affected the lives and futures of individuals forever. We too are to know this love, not just intellectually *know*, but to experience,[12] inhale, ingest, this love. To be found in His love, and His love to be found in us.

As we move into discovering more about the surprising power of joy, we must be anchored in the certainty that joy has its beginning in God—that it is an inseparable part of who He is, and an overflow into our lives of Him just being Himself. Our God sings over people, cities and nations, delights in the undelightful, and has moved toward us in unconditional, unfathomable love. This is the only place to start. This is the root of all joy.

• • •

REDISCOVERING JOY: STEP 2

Engage in Prayer

> *Father, I acknowledge and receive You as the great God of Joy, and lean in now to the reality of Your joy that is so evident in our world. All of creation speaks of Your incredible goodness, love, and joyful intent. As I make more room for Your joy, I welcome You to reteach me what it means to live in and experience the joy that only comes from You. Father, I let go of any beliefs that have shut out or shut down joy as irrelevant, impossible to find, or less spiritual, and I jump into Your abundant joy today, wanting everything that You have made available, and the fullness of joy that You are bringing into my life. In the all-powerful name of Jesus.*

Reflection

- Take time to reflect upon how easy it is for you to receive the Father as a God of Joy.
- Reflect upon a time when you encountered creation in a powerful way. What emotions or

memories do you carry from that experience? Spend some time remembering as many details as possible from that moment, making room for His joy.

- Set aside an hour of time to be alone with God. Ask Him what He thinks about you and how He sees you. Be ready to make note of everything that He shares with you. Receive His delight in you and His Father's love for you.

Activation

- Take time to craft a prayer-declaration using Scripture and the chapter content. Include the phrase "God delights in me" throughout and release this daily as a proclamation.

- Intentionally share about God's joy with those in your sphere of influence. Not preaching at them, but instead inviting conversation about who He is as our God of joy.

- Make a decision that the culture of your own heart and the culture where you have influence would be a "no orphan" zone and reflect core values that promote this.

3

The Ultimate Joy Giver

From the first biblical predictions and promises made about Jesus, to the message of His immanent birth, joy was evident and amplified in the announcements. He was the One who was sent to change everything, and He did. Jesus came into our world and brought the Father's joy with Him:

> *But the angel said to them, "Do not be afraid. I bring you good news that will cause great joy for all the people. ... Glory to God in the highest heaven, and on earth peace to those on whom his favor rests"* (Luke 2:10,14 NIV).

It's crucial for us to look into this annually quoted passage and let the joy factor impact us. The angels are announcing good news that will cause *great joy* for all people. It was the beginning of the end of the dominance of darkness, and the beginning of the beginning of a new epoch of history. The message was global in scope—for all people—and promised peace here on earth because God's favor rests on us. This is wonderful to me.

The Father announced that His *favor rested* over humanity when we were still separated, still enemies, still violently opposed to Him and His ways.

Love was speaking and love was acting. Grasping the wonder of this is transformational. Not inviting us to a walk of shame back to Him, but a decided favor that *moved toward* us. It is not difficult to see why the Father and all of Heaven were excited about the arrival. The plan of Jesus coming was conceived in joy, He was announced in joy, and arrived carrying joy. He represented the fulfillment of the joyful expectation that death itself would be defeated forever, that Eden living would be restored, and God would inherit a new family of sons and daughters for eternity.

In time, when Jesus was to begin to represent the Father and His Kingdom, His job description in Luke 4:18-19 was packed full of joy moments waiting to happen. Jesus said,

> *The Spirit of the LORD is upon Me, because He has anointed Me to preach the gospel to the poor; He has sent me to heal the brokenhearted, to proclaim liberty to the captives and recovery of sight to the blind, to set at liberty those who are oppressed; to proclaim the acceptable year of the LORD* (Luke 4:18-19).
>
> *The Spirit of the Lord is upon me, and he has anointed me to be hope for the poor, freedom for the brokenhearted, and new eyes for the blind, and to preach to prisoners, "You are set free!" I have come to share the message of Jubilee, for the time of God's great acceptance has begun* (Luke 4:18-19 TPT).

The corresponding Old Testament passage in Isaiah 61 also carries great implications for joy:

> *To proclaim the year of the LORD's favor and the day of vengeance of our God, to comfort all who mourn, and provide for those who grieve in Zion, to bestow on them a crown of beauty instead of ashes, the oil of joy instead of mourning, and a garment of praise instead of a spirit of despair...* (Isaiah 61:2-3 NIV).

These are well-known truths to believers, but the multipliers of joy are sometimes missed. Again, the favor of God shows up in reference to Jubilee[1]—a time of celebration, canceled debts, and release for prisoners. Jesus came to announce an epoch of God's favor as well as vengeance against *everything* that *had oppressed people.* The brokenhearted become "whole hearted," and captives are freed from prison. If we think about this in a real-world situation, these are massively joyful outcomes. The spiritually and naturally blind get to see again, and those who grieve are comforted and given a crown of beauty for things that were so desecrated that only ashes remained. I want you to imagine this for a moment. This is raw material for a lot of joy!

Then there is more—instead of despair and mourning, there will be joy and praise. Oil poured out and a garment to wear. Holy Spirit introduces Himself here; He is in the middle of this glorious transformation. He is the oil in Scripture and the garment we are to permanently wear.

We have discovered that joy is an undisputed attribute of God, and Jesus the Joy Giver is *just like* His Father, revealing joyful intentions and planning for joyful reunions with those whom He had created. Time after time in Scripture, explosions of joy happened in response to Jesus revealing the Father—changing people's lives with outrageous acceptance, inconceivable restoration, and extravagant healing.

> ...*the Son can do nothing by Himself; he can only do what he sees his Father doing, because whatever the Father does the Son also does. For the Father loves the Son and shows him all he does* (John 5:19-20).

Jesus, doing the work of the Father, reached into undeserving, chaotic, and "unclean" lives and kissed them with grace. The fact that these miracles were often *unexpected and undeserved* make it all the more inconceivable for those who received them, and all the more beautiful for us to imagine. How would it feel to be set free from a lifetime of infirmity, or to be finally healed after many years of people crying "unclean" as you walked by them because of the uncurable leprosy you carried visibly?[2] I want us to move past a head response for a moment, and move into our hearts.

We often imaginatively read about the paralyzed man whose friends lowered him through the roof to be touched by Jesus.[3] Truthfully, the focus is often more on the complexity of the roof invasion than the man's brokenness. Jesus radically forgives the man's spiritual sickness by announcing *forgiveness,* which fiercely angers the Pharisees and teachers of the law, and then *totally restores* the man's body. I often imagine what it was like for him, for *everything* to change in one moment.

The account of the famous jumping and leaping man who the disciples healed in Acts 3:8, also captures me. He is often more well known as the character in a children's church song than a picture of the explosive joy that is present and available every-where because the Kingdom of God is with us, upon us, and in us. Let's take off our 21st-century quiet-time lens for a moment and place ourselves within the story, stepping away from our tamed expectations that often rush past the moment. This man, who had been crippled from *birth*, when *totally healed*, was filled with inexplicable, uncontainable, and dare we say, uncontrollable joy. Not an intellectual response, not a thought-through rehearsed running and leaping, not a calculated lifting of one hand in wor-ship on a Sunday morning. Rather, it was a running over into the streets, explosively large, changing the atmosphere sort of joy. He was literally jumping, leaping, and praising God. Those who had known him all of his life as the begging cripple now saw him whole and transformed, and full of joy. Who would not have smiled? Who would not have beamed and laughed with wonder?

I imagine my mouth would have dropped open without my permission as it did at the sight of the Grand Canyon. Maybe a cheer and a shout would have spontaneously jumped out. These are the works of Jesus. This is the heart of the joy-filled Father. The ramifications for the man's future were huge. Everything would be different. Socially, financially, relationally, physically, mentally, emotionally. Do you get it? Changed forever. How else was he supposed to respond? What a beautiful thing to experi-ence. Jesus the Joy Giver does it again.

Then there is the woman caught in adultery,[4] with no excuse and no escape until Jesus extends a new type of mercy that is other-worldly, and culturally impossible—lifting her and her accusers to another level. The widow of Nain's[5] only son is given back to her as Jesus' compassion breaks through the final word of death, turning the deepest sorrow into the highest hope. The woman who had been bleeding consistently for twelve years[6] and spent everything to find a cure, experiences the power of proximity to Jesus, and the secret sickness is healed.

The myriad of difficulty, pain, and sorrow interwoven in these and so many other stories of Jesus' intervention is heartbreaking. These were socially, physically, financially, emotionally catastrophic circumstances, and Jesus simply reverses them. In many translations, the words "filled with awe"[7] describe what follows when experiencing these amazing moments. Awe conjures up a sense of amazement, sudden astonishment, and wonder.

"Wonder" is also something we need to recapture and reclaim. It is a younger sibling of joy. When we are full of wonder, unjaded innocence is present, and we trust innocently again in something or someone, expansive, who is not only powerful, but loves to surprise us, and loves to continually do wonder-filled things. *Joy and wonder are never far away when the Father is doing what comes naturally to Him.*

So, we have made room for the God who brings joy to crippled places. But what about the rebellious, stinking, prodigal places? Can we make room for the Father who responds in joy to that? The parable of the prodigal son[8] is actually a story that speaks more about the outrageously loving Father than the rebellious son. It is actually a parable that reveals how good God is, rather than how bad the son was. But the latter is where we usually place our focus. In the biblical story, what is the father's response when he sees the son coming a long way off? He *runs* to him and kisses him; and after giving him back the robe and ring, which symbolize both his identity and authority in the family, the father threw a party. He initiated a celebration—a joy-filled family feast where the fattened calf was slaughtered and the celebration of the restored son was paramount.

Here again we are confronted with a God of lavish joy who loves to give it away. Jesus was deliberately telling an outrageous story to give us a glimpse into just how loving, wonderful, and joyful our heavenly Father actually is. Remember that Jesus both *taught and demonstrated*. He loved to show and tell to reveal the Father: God is really, really good, so let me *show you* Him restoring the physically and emotionally crippled and oppressed to wholeness and dignity, because that's what He loves to do.

Do you know that we are the recipients of joy here, not only because we are all prodigal in comparison to the ways of God, but because He is infinitely good and has determined in advance the antidote of our fallenness, which has been overwhelmed by His joy-filled goodness. I am stating this again and again for a reason. Total provision has been made for us to no longer live starved of the revelation knowledge of God as the God of joy. We have been undernourished and depleted in our experiential understanding of the God of richest joy and laughter. As those created in His image, we get to laugh because He does. He is gloriously holy, and wonderfully fearful, and filled with light, *but also* the Author of joy. He is, in fact, the original laughter.

> *But about the Son he says...“You have loved righteousness and hated wickedness; therefore God, your God, has set you above your companions by anointing you with the oil of joy”* (Hebrews 1:8-9 NIV).
>
> *But about his Son, he called him “God,” saying...“For you have cherished righteousness and detested lawlessness.*

For this reason, God, your God, has anointed you and poured out the oil of bliss on you more than on any of your friends" (Hebrews 1:9 TPT).

It is clear here in Hebrews, that Jesus was anointed with joy by the Father! In loving righteousness and hating wickedness, joy was given that differentiated Him above others. The Passion Translation (TPT) says the "oil of bliss" was poured out upon Him. Jesus loved righteousness and was also blissfully joyful at the same time. I love this word picture. My friend Georgian Banov likes to say that the world and religion have two separate agendas: the world wants us to be happy, and religion wants us to be holy—but the Father enables both; He loves to make us both happy and holy.

In that same hour he rejoiced in the Holy Spirit and said, "I thank you, Father, Lord of heaven and earth, that you have hidden these things from the wise and understanding and revealed them to little children..." (Luke 10:21 ESV).

This Scripture verse gives us another glimpse into the joy that Jesus carried. The seventy disciples had just returned from being sent and were full of joy because demons were submitting to the name of Jesus. After adjusting their mindset a little, and turning them toward their heavenly citizenship, Jesus erupts with joy. The root word[9] for *rejoiced* here means "to *jump for joy* and be exceedingly glad." A related Hebrew word for *rejoice* means "to *spin around* under the influence of violent emotion." Jesus became really joyful when the childlike caught the revelation of the Kingdom. Again, we can so easily interpret the words that

Jesus says as somber in tone. But Scripture records that it was in the *context of exceeding joy* that Jesus celebrated childlike faith.

> *Learn this well: Unless you dramatically change your way of thinking and become teachable and learn about heaven's kingdom realm with the wide-eyed wonder of a child, you will never be able to enter in* (Matthew 18:3 TPT).

In His birth and in every assignment from the Father, we see Jesus demonstrating joy. From turning water into wine, multiplying loaves and fish, stilling storms and raising the dead, He created moments of wonder and joy that revealed more of the Father's nature and His ways. It is overwhelmingly powerful to see that joy was also consistent even as He contemplated His death on the cross:

> *Looking unto Jesus the author and finisher of our faith; who for the joy that was set before him endured the cross, despising the shame, and is set down at the right hand of the throne of God* (Hebrews 12:2 KJV).

Another translation says, "for the joy of obtaining the prize."[10] When we understand that the joy set before Him was us, the prize that the Father sent Him to redeem, then this truth comes alive and is greatly humbling. A greater prize enabled Jesus to despise the torture, humiliation, shame, and excruciating pain of the cross.

We will look at joy in the middle of suffering in a later chapter. But in this moment, let the truth that a greater joy was set before Him—the entire redemption, reconciliation, and transformation of the entire human race forever. It was us.

Joy focuses on a greater goal, a greater prize, a superior outcome than the present, without denying reality, and is fuel to continue to walk through whatever is between us and the revealed will of God.

> *Most assuredly, I say to you that you will weep and lament, but the world will rejoice; and you will be sorrowful, but your sorrow will be turned into joy. ... Therefore you now have sorrow; but I will see you again and your heart will rejoice, and your joy no one will take from you* (John 16:20,22).
>
> *Let me make it quite clear: You will weep and be overcome with grief over what happens to me. The unbelieving world will be happy, while you will be filled with sorrow. But know this, your sadness will turn into joy when you see me again! ...And then your hearts will burst with joy, with no one being able to take it from you!* (John 16:20,22 TPT)

The most costly event in history—the sacrifice of the life and righteousness of the Son of God—gave way to the greatest event in history, the resurrection of the Christ! The "It is finished" was pronounced not only over sin and separation of humanity from God, but over the power of death, hell, the grave, and the authority of satan and his kingdom, totally and forever. Jesus' birth released joy, His life and assignments released joy, and His death and resurrection purchased and sealed victory forever, releasing a joy into our lives that can never be taken from us. It is really important for us to hear and understand this truth. The resurrection has secured our joy forever; it's no longer based on anything that *we* can do or have to do. The highway from the Father to His children is open, based on the completed work of the Son. Joy is ours, purchased with blood. Sealed with the defeat of death itself.

> *Though you have not seen him, you love him; and even though you do not see him now, you believe in him and are filled with an inexpressible and glorious joy* (1 Peter 1:8 NIV).

Here, Peter highlights *normality* for us as believers and the recipients of resurrection life. *Inexpressible and glorious joy.* We believe in Him and are now inhabited by His very Spirit. Jesus was getting at something really profound when He said that it would be to our advantage that He went away.[11] No one imagined that the Spirit of God would literally take up residence in every child of God as a Friend and Guide and fill us with inexpressible and glorious joy. As those who ourselves were crippled and prodigal in multiple ways and have been lifted by love, now simply love Him back and believe—and we are encountered and marked by joy. But not just touched by an occasional drop.

As First Peter 1:8 reveals, part of our experiential inheritance is to be *filled* with joy. Reading this, we resonate with and are reminded of the reality of the joy that is already operating within us. Jesus, the resurrection and the life, is the Source, the One who fills His Church with joy. Not just a measure to get us through, not simply a portion that meets need. All of this and more. We are *filled*, which implies that there is no more room. Abundant. Enough. Joy to capacity. Aligning with the reality of the Kingdom reveals to us that every provision has been made for us as those who walk with Jesus. We are not working *for joy,* or only receiving it as an afterglow for doing good works. We are in fact filled to capacity with joy when we spend ourselves on loving Him. Resting in His finished and complete work.

However, Peter is reminding us that this is not ordinary joy—it is described as inexpressible and glorious. This is joy with additions. A joy that is not easy to define or to express, a joy that is not easily described, a joy that is glorious. This is the joy-potency that is available to us in Christ. There are a few things accessible to us in life that can be described as inexpressible and glorious. Maybe we could try and make a list. It would probably be different for each of us.

Maybe you are captivated by beautiful sun-swept beaches, ancient architecture, the sunrise over a mountain range, or the food craft of a Michelin Star chef. But in honesty, what can be compared to Him? Even so, the Church has not typically celebrated and made room for *joy* that is inexpressible and glorious. What comes to mind if I asked you to imagine and describe inexpressible and glorious joy? Intense laughter, gregarious smiling, explosive emotion, speechless adulation? Yes, all of this. Jesus has expanded the bandwidth capacity of our joy. He has already made a way for His joy to be resident in us. Because of what has already been done for us, we get to daily enjoy and experience dimensions of His joy that were there from eternity past and encounter them now in the reality of the present.

A Kingdom has been transferred to us through a faithful, joyful King. Jesus reclaimed us with His own life, and in the process *reclaimed joy* for all of us, and all who will come. He sent His early followers to continue what He had started and empowered them from the inside out. It has now been transferred to us, and we are the ones invited, in our generation, to steward and demonstrate this wonder-filled and joyful Kingdom.

• • •

REDISCOVERING JOY: STEP 3

Engage in Prayer

> *Jesus, thank You for revealing the Father to us and showing us what a life overtaken by the Holy Spirit looks like. You came to us and for us carrying the Father's joy and released joy to everyone You encountered. Thank You for the inexpressible and glorious joy that lives in me now, because You made a way back to relationship with the Father. I acknowledge every place I have toned down, minimized, or leaned into religiosity regarding how You walked with the Father. You are the ultimate Joy Giver. You live in me. As I become more like You, thank You I was created to give away Your ultimate joy to see people You love awaken to who You really are. I receive the oil of joy today, in a new dimension, more lavishly than I ever have before.*

Reflection

- Revisit some of Jesus' key miracles, signs, and wonders in Scripture. Take time to really place yourself inside the story. Resist the usual way you have approached the story and imagine what truly happened. Allow the sights, smells, emotions, words, and interactions within the text to impact you. Make room for new revelation and insight that Holy Spirit is wanting to bring.

- Spend some time evaluating the level of wonder you have allowed yourself to experience recently. Have you moved away from childlikeness? What steps are you supposed to take to recapture wonder in God?

Activation

- Take time to allow the Holy Spirit to minister to any places where you are brokenhearted, oppressed, or captive. Jesus is still setting people free, and that includes you. Your inheritance includes freedom from anything that attempts to steal, kill, or destroy. Take responsibility for any decisions you made that have led to captivity. Run to the Father and receive freedom and healing.

- Make a list of times you have received Luke 4:18-19 from Jesus. Remember what He has done and thank Him for every area that you have experienced transformation. Practice gratitude in prayer daily to develop a lifestyle of thankfulness, even before you see change in areas that may be challenging.

4

A Joyful Kingdom

Jesus preached and demonstrated His Father's Kingdom—the King's domain—God's rule and ways released over His universe. He told stories to help us understand how it works and what it is like. He taught His disciples to pray that it would come on earth, gave them keys to unlock it,[1] and consistently released it into people's lives. References to the Kingdom are found throughout the New Testament. You can study it for yourself. When the Kingdom shows up, bodies are healed, the dead are raised, the power of sin is eradicated, dignity is restored, people fall in love with God, and the supernatural invades the natural. Because you are reading this book, you have probably also experienced the manifestation of the Kingdom of God and been a recipient of its power and joy.

When we think in terms of God and His Kingdom, everything has a place; like an overarching framework, it gives us context for everything that God does. Every theme and distinctive in Scripture is important; but if we build churches focused only on a particular emphasis, we inevitably experience only a portion of the Kingdom. However, when we build focused upon the entire Kingdom, there is room for everything that God wants to release to us to be actualized.

As the Church, we have often ignored the Kingdom or interpreted every Scripture about the Kingdom as referring to a time in the *future* when we will go to Heaven. My purpose here is not an in-depth study because many others have already done this wonderfully; however, as we look at the numerous Scriptures, it is impossible to make the Kingdom of God fit neatly into a box of only a future heavenly reality. I believe that God's Kingdom actually functions *past, present, and future,* just like God Himself. The Kingdom of God is simply a description of what we encounter when He is simply being Himself, His magnanimous reign and all of the benefits and wonders of it.

The King's domain was active in eternity past, is moving in the present, and will be there in the future, into eternity. What that means for us is that we don't have to put the power and presence of the Kingdom into a future time, we can live and operate in it now. Jesus, in teaching His disciples to pray at their request, offered them wisdom to ask, "Your Kingdom come, Your will be done on *earth* as it is in Heaven." The Kingdom is clearly a now Kingdom, as well as a future Kingdom.

Let's take a deeper look at the Romans passage referred to in the opening section of the book. It has an interesting emphasis that is powerful to understand:

> *For the kingdom of God is not a matter of eating and drinking, but of righteousness, peace and joy in the Holy Spirit* (Romans 14:17 NIV).

This is not a complicated passage. The context is the Kingdom, the result is righteousness, peace, and joy—and the vehicle is the Holy Spirit. These are three catalytic elements described as coming together to release how God's Kingdom works and what it produces. They are also three foundational aspects of life in God that the Church often overlooks and sometimes even purposefully deemphasizes.

It's my observation that there are some believers who love to talk about advancing the Kingdom, but don't want to include joy; and there are others who are Holy Spirit joy-junkies who do not want to reach beyond the well-being of their own soul and see God's Kingdom change others. There are also those who like to talk a great deal about standards of righteousness, but neglect the person of the Holy Spirit and joy; and there are some who will do anything to build a framework of peace at any cost, but neglect righteousness. What if the Kingdom—righteousness, peace, joy, and the Holy Spirit—could all coexist in the same space? God seems to think so.

Paul is simply saying that the Kingdom is not a matter of natural means or the keeping of rituals, but in the evidence of righteousness, peace, and joy. That's a very interesting statement that gives us a definitive measure. Joy is described as one-third of the Kingdom; so logically, where the Kingdom is manifest there will be joy; and where the God kind of joy is manifest, there is the Kingdom.

Clearly the Kingdom of God is not only made up of these three components, but Paul helps us make a course correction regarding what the Kingdom of God is like, and what its fruit is. The Kingdom is a kingdom that manifests joy. Period. Stop and think about this for a moment. This may be a renewing-of-your-mind moment, or an opportunity to go deeper. Let's add this to our declarations, "Joy is normal in God's Kingdom." Say it out loud. Maybe shout it. "Joy is normal in God's Kingdom!"

I want to present to you that joy is often a forgotten pillar, a neglected catalyst in the work of God even though it is an evident and consistent presence in the person of the Father. You may have noticed that I am reemphasizing joy for you *over and over again,* in multifaceted ways, so that it saturates your thoughts. We are in the process of deconstructing mindsets formed in the Church that have produced a restricted place of influence for the potent power of joy.

The opposite of righteousness, peace, and joy is unrighteousness, chaos, and sorrow. We see a lot of that in people's lives and in our nations. Let us mandate to banish these things everywhere we walk; and that instead, the God of joy and the joy of God would be seen, felt, experienced, and fully known. Jesus helps us understand that walking in the influence of this Kingdom of joy isn't something that we have to strive for or earn: "…it is your Father's good pleasure to give you the kingdom," says Jesus in Luke 12:32.

God has given the Kingdom to us. A powerful Kingdom. A transformative Kingdom. A joyful Kingdom. The same Kingdom that Jesus released. What would it look like for us to live as if the Father out of *good pleasure* had given us His Kingdom to manifest? Lavish. Enough for all. No lack. More than enough to give away. But what does stewarding and releasing it look like?

First, we get to do what Jesus did,[2] which is amazing in itself. Second, we have been given several overarching mandates[3] that solidify for us what releasing the Kingdom looks like. Let's review:

1. *Creation Mandate—Genesis 1:26-28 (ESV)*

    Then God said, "Let us make man in our image, after our likeness. And let them have dominion over the fish of the sea and over the birds of the heavens and over the livestock and over all the earth and over every creeping thing that creeps on the earth." So God created man in his own image, in the image of God he created him; male and female he created them. And God blessed them. And God said to them, "Be fruitful and multiply and fill the earth and subdue it, and have dominion over the fish of the sea and over the birds of the heavens and over every living thing that moves on the earth."

2. *Jesus' Mission Statement—Luke 4:18-19 (ESV)*

    The Spirit of the Lord is upon me, because he has anointed me to proclaim good news to the poor. He has sent me to proclaim liberty to the captives and recovering of sight to the blind, to set at liberty those who are oppressed, to proclaim the year of the Lord's favor.

3. *The Great Commission—Mark 16:15-18 (ESV)*

    Go into all the world and proclaim the gospel to the whole creation. Whoever believes and is baptized will be saved, but whoever does not believe will be condemned. And these signs will accompany those who believe: in my name they will cast out demons; they will speak in new tongues; they will pick up serpents with their hands; and if they drink any deadly poison, it will not hurt them; they will lay their hands on the sick, and they will recover.

4. Discipling Nations—Matthew 28:18-20

All authority in heaven and on earth has been given to me. Go therefore and make disciples of all nations, baptizing them in the name of the Father and of the Son and of the Holy Spirit, teaching them to observe all that I have commanded you. And behold, I am with you always, to the end of the age.

These scriptural mandates provide us with overarching vision for what we as the Church have been sent and equipped to do. Part of the joy of extending the Kingdom in these ways is manifesting the finished work of Jesus. We are called into partnership with God based on an already accomplished end. Essentially, we are part of a massive cleanup operation. Operating *out of* a change of covenant because of the finished work of Jesus[4] is one of the greatest shifts we need to make as the Church.

Much of where we get stuck is through neglecting to relate to our world through the reality that Jesus has *already* won. This leaves us fighting *for* victory, instead of *from* it. Remember, the death, resurrection, and ascension of Jesus has obliterated the kingdom of darkness, death, hell, and the grave and opened a highway for transformation and the Spirit of God to be resident in us with a joy that can never be taken from us.

Isaiah 61 contains rich content regarding the operation of joy and the Kingdom, and uses the language of redemption, transformation, and upgrade mentioned in the opening chapter.

As we revisit the passage that describes Jesus' job description and continue reading, it opens out for us who *we are* in this meta-narrative and gives us solid indicators of what our role is in manifesting this joyful Kingdom:

> *To grant [consolation and joy] to those who mourn in Zion—to give them an ornament (a garland or diadem) of beauty instead of ashes, the oil of joy instead of mourning, the garment [expressive] of praise instead of a heavy, burdened, and failing spirit—that they may be called oaks of righteousness [lofty, strong, and magnificent, distinguished for uprightness, justice, and right standing with God], the planting of the Lord, that He may be glorified. ...Instead of your [former] shame you shall have a two-fold recompense; instead of dishonor and reproach [your people] shall rejoice in their portion. Therefore in their land they shall possess double [what they had forfeited]; everlasting joy shall be theirs* (Isaiah 61:3,7 AMPC).

There is an amazing transition revealed here. We are transformed from being individuals who are broken, oppressed, bound, and burdened, to being *planted by God* as oaks of righteousness described as strong and distinguished for uprightness and justice. Former shame is upgraded to a double blessing and everlasting joy is thrown in for good measure! This is astounding. The Message translation of the Bible says, "...Because you got a double dose of trouble and more than your share of contempt, your inheritance in the land will be doubled and your joy go on forever" (Isaiah 61:7 MSG). God loves to restore double in His goodness what was stolen from us in darkness.

But there is more.

REBUILD, RESTORE, RENEW

And they shall rebuild the old ruins, they shall raise up the former desolations, and they shall repair the ruined cities, the desolations of many generations (Isaiah 61:4).

They will rebuild the ancient ruins and restore the places long devastated; they will renew the ruined cities that have been devastated for generations (Isaiah 61:4 NIV).

Out of a context of joyful personal transformation, we become those who are *not only recipients* of massive restoration, but those who *carry and execute a restorative process for others.* I want you to notice the words *rebuild, restore, and renew.* These words speak to a renovating back to previous purpose, through a process, where the final result is as good as new.

This King's domain that we steward miraculously restores not only individuals, but systems, societal infrastructure, regions, and geographic areas. Ancient ruins, places long devastated, and ruined cities are rebuilt, renewed, and restored. A context of joy enables us to pronounce and prophesy a preferable future over what has been diminished in design or purpose. Joy announces the hope of a different future.

It seems to me that we are in a transition in the Body of Christ and in this season are prophetically living in between verses 3 and

4 in Isaiah 61. Meaning, that we are situated in our generation between *receiving* and *executing changes*. We are to consistently dig into personal renewal and restoration—the Kingdom coming *to me*, while at the same time stretching into corporate rebuilding and restoration—the Kingdom moving *through me*. God is orchestrating an addition to the signs and wonders movement that ministers to *the individual*, by activating a restoration and reformation movement that ministers to *infrastructure and culture*. Again, out of a context of joy, we are to rebuild, renew, and restore in unapologetic ways.

The nature of the Giver who lives in us requires that we become distributors, not merely consumers of the goodness of His Kingdom. This is done in the spirit of royalty disguised as servants. Jesus was clear that greatness in the Kingdom is defined by servanthood, an intentional posture from an identity of sonship:

> *But Jesus called them to Himself and said, "You know that the rulers of the Gentiles lord it over them, and those who are great exercise authority over them. Yet it shall not be so among you; but whoever desires to become great among you, let him be your servant. And whoever desires to be first among you, let him be your slave"* (Matthew 20:25-27).

Transforming culture as secure sons and daughters who serve; lending our newfound strength to others to see a rebuilding, restoring, and renewing according to God's blueprints and design. I believe that those who have been faithful to serve individuals will be invited to serve cities. Because we are no longer afraid of our own darkness, we will not be afraid of the darkness manifested in our streets and communities, realizing that all of us, in our darkest places are mirroring what we are actually called to in our most fruitful.[5]

What if fear and darkness actually mapped out places we should engage and not avoid? Where places of harvest are marked by stolen joy, highlighting the very places to which the Father is attracted. With this perspective, just like the lepers whom Jesus touched, we will run to the "unclean" less concerned about becoming defiled, and wildly expectant for the opportunity for life to flow, and lives to be changed. Being people God can trust is the endgame in stewarding His Kingdom; and so we get to ask what Father wants, and how He wants to do it, and when. Then we get to do it. Full of joy.

As we come to the conclusion of this section, we can say confidently that joy is a gift given to us by Father out of His own consistent supply of joy. Not a fleeting feeling but a potent force that restores us personally, and then propels us to see others restored. Supplied to us unreservedly and without lack, the present and future joy of God is alive and active to alter the generational course of history.

JOY CATALYSTS

If we are to accept the invitation to the mandates listed earlier, we will need access to the supernatural power of joy that we have been exploring. My simple working definition of "supernatural" is the necessary demonstration of God's "super" over our "natural." In every sphere of influence, God's joy-filled Kingdom is sweeping through dark and dusty devastated places, bringing strategies for restoring, architectural blueprints for rebuilding, and inspiration for renewing. Nations are to be discipled *from* joy and *in* joy, one person, one family, one sector, and one sphere at a time.

Rebuilding, restoring, and renewing is contagious. It releases Kingdom endorphins to see God's goodness and joy move and change lives, and then become a catalyst for the multiplication of more joy. Over and over again, His wonders simply cause joy-responses to erupt in people, which then come back to Him in worship, gratitude, and thanks. Maybe this is what we were made to be part of?

I am personally aware of hundreds of stories and testimonies of God's goodness, miracles, and intervention in people's lives. We celebrate and honor these as part of stewarding what God has done and is doing, strengthening ourselves in what He is up to and focusing on His ways and intent. In this section, I focus on some stories of cultural transformation that come from the place of joyful vision and are producing amazing joy-filled results.

A friend of mine owns and operates one of the fastest growing real estate corporations in the United States. His story spanning thirteen years is one of focused dedication, setbacks, detailed diligence, study, the leading of Holy Spirit, supernatural favor, and tremendous hard work, which has resulted in astounding success by the world's standards. Partnering a love for Jesus with business acumen, the vision was to restore some of the most failing apartment complexes in the region and restore them to places where people would want to live, while producing financial prosperity. A win-win model.

Today in this single corporation, hundreds are employed, and income is generated for lawyers, accountants, landscape suppliers and crews, design and construction companies, architects, property management teams, administrators, appliance manufacturers, hardware suppliers, branding and marketing consultants, investors, commercial real estate brokers, cleaning crews, telecommunications and Wi-Fi providers, and all of the subsidiaries and downline of every industry listed. All while restoring, rebuilding, and renewing apartments in need of restoration, and seeing them transformed into contemporary living spaces that provide former residents with upgraded homes, and attract investment and community to both established and regentrified areas of the city. The unlovely is transformed, creativity is maximized, positive home environments are created, and millions of dollars are generated and distributed. That is the Kingdom in operation. Joyful vision with joyful outcomes.

As I was writing this section, a friend of mine in another city posted online, bringing attention to a story of a single mom working as a waitress who had recently served a table of very demanding people. Their generous gift to her was a tiny tip along with an invitation to their church, and a harsh complaint to the manager, which caused her to lose her job. Needless to say, a group of strangers decided to respond and began sending her random tips and words of encouragement through a smartphone app.

As I thought about the situation, I sensed a Holy Spirit nudge, but more than that, a brewing excitement about what this would mean for her and her perception of the Father. Not being able to control what the people in the restaurant did, there were two choices: either posting an injustice rant online or stepping out and partnering with God to reveal Him in a greater way.

Admittedly, sometimes an injustice rant is necessary, especially when your coffee has not been brewed perfectly by a barista. Joking aside, my point here is that I was simply being invited into a joy moment with God, and that this is how we *get to live* every day. The rising joy and anticipation I felt was not intellectually motivated, it was gut-level, intuitive, and emotive—led by Holy Spirit. After following through and sending the amount that was on my heart, the experience continued. I felt a "yes" in my spirit, a pleasure, a rest, a joy that was in the atmosphere that made me smile for the rest of the morning.

The point is not for me to share a random act of kindness that I gallantly responded to, but to describe a joy-process that was too invaluable to miss. There has been a wave of random acts of kindness sweeping through culture. People have picked up on it in the past few years. Paying for the coffee of the person behind you in the drive-through line, covering the restaurant bill for someone at another table. These are manifestations of love and kindness that come from joyful expectation, and a desire to see it released in others.

As I've described to you, there is something wonderful about the joy that rises along with the thought of stepping out and being a blessing to someone for no other reason than just because. It's like a sideswipe of kindness that sneaks up on someone unexpectedly. Just like darkness likes to do, but in reverse. People are literally battered and numbed by numerous assaults from the father of lies whose job description is to steal, kill, and destroy. It's his nature, and everything that looks remotely like stealing, killing, and destroying has its origin in him.

But our Father perpetuates life in abundance—what Jesus said He came to give us.[6] We get to respond when the Father wants to do something extravagant and lavish—we get to be a catalyst for joy in the life of the person who unexpectedly and often undeservedly gets to receive it—and this then perpetuates more joy in us. It's almost as though the Father has set in motion His Church as a perpetual joy machine that gives, receives, catalyzes, magnifies, and multiplies joy wherever it finds itself led by Him.

The women's cautious smile revealed something that she was deeply ashamed of. Living on a literal mountain of trash in a tent, surrounded by children rummaging through the garbage to find items to resell, her hospitality challenged us. She had eagerly invited us into her makeshift home, made of sticks and cloth, to drink tea with her. One of our spiritual fathers had taken our youth group to the Philippines. This was the same trip where my wife and I were engaged, and I taught my first worship-equipping class to an unsuspecting church; my hope is that they have recovered from it.

The natural beauty of the islands, and the warmth and relationally driven Filipino people impacted many of us. I had traveled internationally before but had not encountered poverty and generosity wrapped up in one package like this. My pastor had asked Holy Spirit that morning for the amount of American dollars he should take with him to give away that day, and in the middle of our conversation he asked our host what her current greatest place of need was.

I watched intently, not imagining what her response would be. As she grinned widely, we learned through our translator shared that she was deeply ashamed of losing her teeth, and that her greatest desire was the restoration of her smile. It would have been a wonderful moment for Jesus to miraculously replace all of her missing teeth, but He chose instead, in this moment, to use generosity. The amount for surgery was the exact amount our pastor carried with him, and one year later a photograph arrived by snail-mail. A picture of our friend and her restored smile. No longer cautious and ashamed. The smile was a boisterous grin, from ear to ear. Beaming. "Look at my teeth." Jesus had restored her joy along with her smile. Still living on the mountain of trash, but with a renewed soul. The beautiful ways of God are seen all over this story. Joy in generosity and simple obedience. Restored dignity through a stranger who knew the Dignity Restorer, and became one himself.

Equipping the underground Church in the Middle East is a huge part of our personal mandate and sphere of influence. Several years ago, during a live broadcasting via satellite into homes across the region, an elderly Middle Eastern lady sat in the studio and prayed intently for us as the program aired. I assumed she was a team member's grandmother who had come to visit; and although I could see that spiritual authority rested on her life, I did not know all there was to know.

A polite conversation and a powerful prayer for us ended her visit, and in conversation afterward I discovered more about this spiritual powerhouse. This veteran of the sex-trafficking industry, involved before it was trending, had rescued thousands of girls from around the globe from sex slavery and owned several commercial jets that were used to drop into nations and rescue groups of the vulnerable and least seen. I cannot imagine the joy-bombs that explode as former slaves are lifted and have the literal opportunity to fly away from captors. Relief, disbelief, tears of joy, laughter, deep gratitude. I imagine lots of joy-filled hugs and some shouts.

No one knows who this woman is. You will not see her on social media, Christian television, in large conferences, or speaking on platforms. She is simply a Jesus hero, following the mandate to bring love and transformation to the world in the power of the Holy Spirit, releasing joy and a celebration of freedom over those who have no power to free themselves. Totally hidden. Forerunning. Amazing. At least to me.

These are the kind of people in diverse ways and in very different spheres of influence who are stewarding this joy-filled Kingdom to rebuild, renew, and restore. Where do you fit into all of this? What is your role? Right where you are, in the opportunities and moments that have been given to you. This is the question we *all* get to ask, because we *all get to play*, and we *all* get to release His joy.

• • •

REDISCOVERING JOY: STEP 4

Engage in Prayer

> *Father, Your Kingdom is not of this world, and is incredible, powerful, and joy filled. Thank You for the righteousness, peace, and joy that is my inheritance in You, that is available permanently, and which You give freely and abundantly. You have changed me and brought transformation, granting me joy, beauty, and double*

honor. Just as You have rebuilt, restored, and renewed me, release me as a restorative catalyst that rebuilds, restores, and renews places long devastated, seeing the generations that are to come reflect You and come into fullness. This is the power of Christ in me, the authority of Your Kingdom, and the privilege of coworking with You in this world. I choose to step into my role as a joy catalyst in every place I see You working and moving, on earth as it is in Heaven.

Reflection

- Reflect on the times that the Kingdom of God showed up and released transformation through the life of Jesus. The places in Scripture that demonstrated the Father's Kingdom as superior to every other kingdom. Storms were stilled, the dead were raised, and food was multiplied. Recount moments where you have witnessed the supernatural Kingdom invade this realm. How do you plan to partner with God to see more? How could everyday life adjust to make room for God's Kingdom intervention?

- Brainstorm what the words *rebuild, restore,* and *renew* mean to you. What redemptive gifts rest upon your life and your family to see devastated places, ruined cities, and desolations reassigned? What new delivery systems does He want to reveal so that you can step into this joyful mandate?

Activation

- Research and ask for Father to reveal initiatives that He wants you to partner with in revealing His joyful Kingdom. He may show you to reengage with a previous activity, partner with your church, start a business, or volunteer with a ministry organization in your city or region. Take off any restrictions and limits and remain open to new opportunities to reveal the Father.

- In the next thirty days, listen for Holy Spirit's leading regarding random acts of kindness. Allow yourself to dream with God. What creative, financial, and other resources has He given you to make a difference in the life of someone else? Don't disregard things that you may think are small or insignificant. He is in the details, and people are changed by Holy Spirit-inspired acts of thoughtful, intentional kindness that disarm and unravel the challenge, frustration, or discouragement that they may be walking through.

5

Inside Out

*...And by this we know that He abides in us,
by the Spirit whom He has given us.*
—1 JOHN 3:24

*T*here are many scriptural truths that describe the inside-out life we experience in God. We often pray and desire Him to come down, and of course He loves to reveal and manifest His presence in unique and powerful ways. There *are dimensions of who He is* that we have not yet seen or experienced. But the reality that His presence lives within us when we are born again—that the Kingdom of righteousness, peace, and joy is actually *within us*—is both a scriptural and experiential reality for us as followers of Jesus:

> *...The kingdom of God does not come with observation.... For indeed, the kingdom of God is within you* (Luke 17:20-21).

The experience of the Christian life is that we are continually learning to cooperate with the internal reality of the God who lives on the inside. The God of joy who has marvelously made His home in us, and our home in Him. What Jesus demonstrated in dynamic authority, vibrant joy, and deep compassion came only from a life lived in intimacy with the Father and the Holy Spirit. What the disciples demonstrated in declaring the good news of the resurrection to thousands, demonstrating signs and wonders, and leading the early Church through great heights and depths, came only from an internal reality that was more vigorous than any outward reality they faced.

In celebrating advancements in the previous chapter, wonderful examples of transformation, I want us to be careful not to advertise or gather around formulas or an end goal, but instead underline that these life-giving initiatives were not a result of just a smart brainstorming session, but from an ongoing, inside-out relational walk with Jesus. The kind of transformation we have been discussing begins with a vibrant inward-cultivated life with God who initiates and brings into reality joyful outcomes for us and our world.

We have looked at the presence of joy in the Father and the Son, and now want to look at the One who makes all that is in the Father available and accessible to us today. The Holy Spirit is probably the most misunderstood and debated person of the Trinity. Not a thing or a force, or an energy—He is *the Person* of the Holy Spirit. He is God's very Spirit, sent to us and living in us. He is the Interface with the Kingdom sent here to be with us, connecting us to the presence of God. He monitors every one of the 7 billion hearts on the planet. That's staggering isn't it? He knows things. He is *the* Expert when it comes to transformation and restoration. From the beginning of creation, He was the One who hovered over the chaos in Genesis 1:1, waiting for the Father to speak, "Let there be light" into the void.

The Holy Spirit then can be thought of as our *Interface* to access everything available in the Father. Everything we will ever need is released to us through Holy Spirit who lives in us. We all resonate with the promise that says God can do "immeasurably more than all we ask or imagine."[1] But we often miss what comes next, "according to His power that is at work *within* us." Everything we experience and receive in God is a by-product of relationship with Holy Spirit and is realized through His presence in us. Not a transaction, a method, a contract, or a clever principle—but the living and active Spirit of God. Over time, this grows to become our unique, bespoke, detailed, particular history with the One who lives in us. Where the cross and resurrection has purchased our entry into the incredible realm of the Kingdom, it is the Holy Spirit who now takes us by the hand to explore the vast dimensions and attributes of what has been made accessible to us.

We are probably familiar with the concept of the fruit of the Spirit. It is contrasted in the book of Galatians with the fruit of the flesh, and gives us a list of attributes:

> *But the fruit of the Spirit is love, joy, peace, patience, kindness, goodness, faithfulness, gentleness, self-control; against such things there is no law* (Galatians 5:22-23 ESV).

But the fruit produced by the Holy Spirit within you is divine love in all its varied expressions: joy that over-flows, peace that subdues, patience that endures, kindness in action, a life full of virtue, faith that prevails, gentleness of heart, and strength of spirit. Never set the law above these qualities, for they are meant to be limitless (Galatians 5:22-23 TPT).

Rather than admirable qualities that we strain to produce, these characteristics of God are cultivated inside us as we give Holy Spirit permission to rule in us and move through us. As we already discovered, this fruit of the Spirit ministers to *us* initially, and only then becomes something we can represent and give away to the world around us. This fruit of the Spirit to us is partly how God restores our soul. His gentleness, patience, kindness, and joy, working inside us, restores us to the person we were always created to be.

We can be sure that the Holy Spirit will always ensure that there is an inside-out, limitless flow of love, joy, peace, patience, kindness, goodness, faithfulness, and self-control. But the *first place* we get to reclaim joy is on the inside. This is sometimes a process, as we have discussed, and requires an honest look at our capacity, ability to receive, and the diversions and distractions that siphon away our joy supply. I believe that it is crucially important to make any adjustments necessary to cultivate a place for the forgotten fruit of joy. We love to celebrate peace and kindness as Christians, which is wonderful. But the element of joy is often neglected, causing us to miss a massive aspect of who God wants to be for us and the world we interface with.

Reclaiming this part of our inheritance starts with us. On the inside. Jesus says:

> *...He who abides in Me, and I in him, bears much fruit; for without Me you can do nothing. If anyone does not abide in Me, he is cast out as a branch and is withered; and they gather them and throw them into the fire, and they are burned. If you abide in Me, and My words abide in you, you will ask what you desire, and it shall be done for you. By this My Father is glorified, that you bear much fruit; so you will be My disciples. As the Father loved Me, I also have loved you; abide in My love. If you keep My commandments, you will abide in My love, just as I have kept My Father's commandments and abide in His love. These things I have spoken to you, that My joy may remain in you, and that your joy may be full* (John 15:5-11).

Jesus' intention for us is to experience joy that is full, and joy that remains. Just as Jesus promised that His peace would remain with us, He has also promised joy. The only condition to this full and remaining joy is continuing connection and relationship with Him. The Bible uses the word *abiding,* meaning to continue in a place, to wait for, to remain stable or fixed, and to endure without yielding.[2] As we remain, the Spirit of God enables a full and remaining joy to grow inside us. *Joy then, this side of Heaven, is not a reward but a result of the inward life of Christ.*

As we navigate daily decisions, the higher invitation is for us to move *from* joy and not *for* joy. Once we have allowed our inward hunger for joy to be met by the Spirit of God and we no longer look for it elsewhere, we are then free to allow our "fullness of joy" to overflow into every aspect of our lives. There is always enough for us and enough to give away. It is not irreverent to lean into more of God's abundant supply of Himself. He initiated the invitation and worked on the Master Plan for millennia. It is not a surprise to Him to have millions of firstborn children all relating to Him, remaining, and pulling on Heaven. He is not running out of love, power, life, light, hope, or joy, so we can rest knowing that what we need to release the Kingdom is available and accessible to us—from the inside out.

> *With joy you will draw water from the wells of salvation* (Isaiah 12:3 ESV).

Scripture points to us accessing joy as part of our salvation inheritance. A source of joy available to us, with a more than enough supply. A "well" implies that there's enough for us to drink, and enough for us to give away, to quench the thirst of a community. Wells are crucial sources of sustenance in many parts of the world even today, and God seems to think that the well of salvation-joy that resides within you is an important source of sustenance in your sphere of influence. We sometimes view salvation in a singular dimension—a ticket to Heaven that acts as our fire insurance—but salvation in a biblical sense implies a wholeness of spirit, soul, and body. Our salvation moment is just the beginning of a journey into discovering all of the Kingdom, and all of the joy that is available.

There are multiple ways in which the presence of God can and does manifest inside us. In a general sense, He is always with us; and in another sense, He manifests Himself specifically in certain moments and circumstances. Part of the joy in eternity will be experiencing the forever revealing of God and who He is. The Bible uses many different word pictures to help spark revelation of the ways in which God's presence moves, works, and manifests. There are many analogies available to us to describe what happens when the finite and the infinite interact. I want to draw attention to three specific ways of looking at God's presence that will help us understand the demonstration of Heaven's joy in and through our lives.

Soaking

Sometimes we encounter God's presence as a soaking experience. These are moments when we sense Him saturating us deeply and gradually, and we experience an incremental soaking. An analogy we can use is *thermal heat* that warms gradually but consistently, heating the deepest layers and remaining long after the source of heat has been removed. There are dimensions of Holy Spirit's anointing and joy that we get to experience like this. Consistent, deep, and soaking.

Moving

In contrast to soaking is an evident moving or flow of God's presence. This is marked by a stirring and flow of intensity and movement. The picture of a river is useful here in that it is sometimes rushing and sometimes gentle, but *always moving*. God's presence and joy turns up and moves like this at times. Cleansing, washing, invigorating, and refreshing.

Explosive

God being God means that He sometimes shows up in an explosive way. These are moments when His presence is not gentle, soaking, or gradual, but immediate, powerful, nuclear in intensity, and at times overwhelming. The analogy here is an *explosion*, a chemical reaction of God's presence made visible, noisy, and transformative—resurrection life that raises dead places and shakes us to the core.

This is by no means an exhaustive list of how God moves, or a definitive explanation of soaking, moving, or explosive places of God's presence, but a lens to look through to help us understand various dimensions of joy that we might encounter and cooperate with as we journey with God.

HOSTING AND LEANING IN

If the presence of God lives in us, then it means that we personally get to host Him, the God of the universe. This is a dangerously wonderful reality and an awe-inspiring privilege.

We have talked lot about making room for joy and making room for God. But how, practically, do we offer God a *personal place* for Him to be Himself?

As those who are filled with Him, we have been drafted into a life marked by *invitation and response*. He invites and we respond. One paradox of the Kingdom is the seeming gap between Him already living in us, and experientially accessing more of His presence. We have received and yet are receiving. We have access, and yet we are leaning in to more. These are all terms of closeness and friendship: hosting, leaning in, access. What others may see as a wasteful use of time, resources, and energy, God may see as a life well spent on hosting His presence, leaning in when He invites, and accessing everything He is offering.[3]

This does not give us permission for irresponsibility toward the commitments and responsibilities that are ours as husbands, wives, parents, leaders, employees, and business owners etc., but challenges us to prioritize the indwelling presence of God, giving Him relational supremacy and the final word in our lives. What does abandoned devotion look like? It is different for each one of us. It is first a position of the heart rather than an outward display of anything that can be measured. First John 2:27 is a key passage of Scripture referring to the indwelling anointing of the Holy Spirit who teaches us:

> *As for you, the anointing [the special gift, the preparation] which you received from Him remains [permanently] in you, and you have no need for anyone to teach you. But just as His anointing teaches you [giving you insight through the presence of the Holy Spirit] about all things, and is true and is not a lie, and just as His anointing has taught you, you must remain in Him [being rooted in Him, knit to Him]* (1 John 2:27 AMP).[4]

The Holy Spirit teaches us all things. He never leaves us, but it is possible for us to lean into or lean out of what He is doing in any given moment. We are invited to live with the permanent questions in our spirit: What are You doing? How can I respond to partner with You in this? Jesus lived in this reality. Doing only what He saw His Father doing and saying only what He heard His Father saying.[5]

Leaning in is a choice, and God will never violate our will. If we are intent on not making room for the joy that is already in us, we may not experience it to the fullest extent. Getting into the flow of what God is doing can be likened to sitting on the edge of a riverbank in a canoe watching the rapids only a short distance away. We are already in the water with *access* to the flow and are experiencing some of the ripple effect of the more turbulent water right where we are—but we are not yet moving with it. *We are not really in.* We still have to cooperate with and move out into the current.

Ezekiel, in his vision-encounter with the river of God,[6] had to respond to multiple invitations to incrementally move out into the deepening water before he accessed the "deep enough to swim in." In one sense there is nothing that we can do to earn access, in another sense we partner in cooperating with what is made available to us.

Just like leaning in, the concept of receiving speaks to repositioning ourselves to accept something that is offered to us that we did not previously have in our possession. It requires a response. We don't supply or demand the gift, but we do cooperate in actively receiving. It requires a choice. The implication of the well-known passage in Ephesians 5:18, "Do not get drunk on wine...but be filled with the Spirit"[7] in the original language refers to an *ongoing* filling, not a one-time event.

The other implication is that just like drinking wine to get drunk, we get filled by receiving and cooperating with drinking of the Spirit. There is an emphasis *placed on us* to receive and to drink. The process may be slightly different for each of us depending on what we have been taught or believed both about God and Holy Spirit. Personally, to receive from God has often meant putting down something else that I'm holding, letting go of my agenda, and admitting that I don't have all of God yet.

The following are values worth considering in positioning ourselves for more of God's presence. They apply whether we are heading out to our local coffee shop, at home with the family, or functioning as a leader of a movement:

- Cultivating an unwavering honor for God being Himself. Living as individuals, churches, environments, and organizations that encourage an atmosphere where God can be Himself.

- Prioritizing relationship with Him as the ultimate priority, above anything that He can do for us.

- An unwavering commitment of love to be someone God can trust with anything—large or small, seen or unseen.

- Pursuing a consistent awareness of His presence—24/7 availability and consciousness of His presence.

- A desire to host Him, making room for Him in whatever way He wants to show up.

- A life that leans in, answering each invitation, however subtle, to ask and understand His purpose and desire.

- Choosing to live on God's timeline, avoiding prioritizing our schedule over His.

- Responding with heartfelt compassion even to whispers, erring on the side of overresponding rather than missing what He wants to do.

These are not laws to follow or scientific methods to implement, but simply suggestions for your heart to begin to make room for more of His presence *on His terms*. You will be astounded at the places in Him and His Kingdom that He will give you access to. Places of His presence that will literally turn your world upside down. It has been my ongoing experience that when God extends access to certain places in Him and His Kingdom, they are available to us again and again. Not presumptuously, but relationally.

Jesus modeled living as a man empowered by and in intimacy with Holy Spirit. He carried authority to displace the demonic, to heal sickness, and to work miracles that reversed or contradicted the natural laws of physics and weather systems. Jesus accessed these places through relationship with the Father and was entrusted with authority at the Father's invitation. It is our privilege as we honor Him just being Himself, to host His presence—receiving and leaning into what He is doing, becoming aware, apprehending, and stepping into what He grants us access to. Welcome to an exciting lifelong journey of discovery.

JOY AND SUFFERING

The term "joy and suffering" sounds like a contradiction, two realities that do not necessarily coexist well together. But it is a paradox of the Kingdom for followers of Jesus, that despite suffering and pain, joy is sustained in our lives from the inside out. There are many more qualified people to write on this subject, who themselves have walked through incredible places of difficulty or persecution, but it is also a crucial issue to address in a book focused on the surprising power of joy.

My wife and I have worked alongside the underground church in the Middle East for more than twenty-five years; it is actually part of her inheritance, growing up in the region as part of a missionary family. Some of the greatest leaders we have ever known have emerged in this context, and steward the massive and sometimes heavy territory they are called to oversee with such joy, that not even residue of the suffering that is a consistent part of the church story there is even noticeable. Jesus has literally become their joy. The One who suffered *for them*, has become the Friend who suffers *with them* through imprisonment, beatings, torture, ridicule, and confiscation of property. Removed from their careers, meeting in secret, family members killed for their faith, and children taken from them. Many who stood through persecution over decades are now seeing a mammoth harvest that is engulfing anything that the spiritual founders of this movement had ever dreamed of. Jesus is receiving the reward of His suffering and they are receiving the joyful fruit of perseverance.

We are not talking about what is sometimes called "persecution" in the West. Not finding the best parking spot and having to walk in the rain is not the devil coming against your life; equally, persecution is not being corrected by your boss because of a really bad work ethic. We are also not referring to a religious spirit that causes us to believe we can *only obtain joy through suffering*, which is a distortion of all that the Joyful One intends for us. This also applies to sickness and disease. God does not send disease upon us as His children in order to test us or grow our joy. However, He is a Father who undoubtedly furnishes us with joy when darkness attempts to steal our health, setting a table for us in the presence of our enemies.[8]

One of the greatest challenges of leadership is calling the Church into more, when we believe we may have already "arrived" at the place of being spiritual giants. God does not despise our weak areas, or our immature areas, but He is not a fan of our pride.

We are facing interesting times in the West, where more than ever being a Christian in the culture or the marketplace sets you apart, is polarizing, and often prompts interesting reactions and responses. How do we stand our ground, maintain our joy, and move through into what God wants to do through us, like the persecuted Church in the Middle East? What will be our response and the outworking of His dealings with us? Preparing a Church that is not prepared to back down and is prepared to suffer, not for themselves but to advance God's desire and purposes. Prepared to continue to manifest Jesus and the power of His Kingdom and being willing to suffer for it. The result is unspeakable and unexpected joy.

> *...you welcomed the message in the midst of severe suffering with the joy given by the Holy Spirit* (1 Thessalonians 1:6 NIV).

A young underground church leader in a country where we work extensively was arrested and interrogated a number of weeks after a training session I had led with several of his church leaders. The network was shaken, many arrested, and the leader was sentenced to five years in prison. His oversight sought God for wisdom as they supported him, and many around the world prayed as he tolerated a year in solitary confinement, and four more years as a prisoner before being released. We had not seen this young leader for over five years and were excited when a series of events enabled us to be reunited with him in his new-found freedom. Throughout his ordeal, the church network had continued to grow, and we had heard updates about him through leaders, but deep down I was not sure what I was going to see when face to face again. Would he be broken? Defeated? Aged beyond recognition? In love with Jesus? Hopeful?

We gathered for a meal with a large group, like family, as is the custom on every and any occasion in the Middle East, and we waited for our guest to arrive. It is not easy to describe the unbridled joy a group of people experience and express when they are reunited with someone they deeply love, who has walked through an extended prison sentence for being their leader. I will let you imagine for yourself.

After the initial, loud, excited reunion, what was astounding to me as the evening progressed was how calm, well-adjusted, peace-filled, and above all, joyful the leader was. He told fascinating stories of how God had met with Him and done outstanding things throughout His time in prison. Watching him laugh, share, and celebrate, as well as cry, was one of the most impacting moments of my journey with the persecuted Church. Only God can supply and preserve joy like this.

Our relationship with the persecuted Church has marked us indelibly and forever. Not only because of their level of sacrifice and deep commitment to Jesus, but because of their contagious joy. The passionate worship and intercession that is a normal part of their lives is fire filled and requires no stirring. It is self-propellant, vibrant, boisterous, unapologetic, and loudly joyful. There are no debates among them about whether God might be offended at their shouts, claps, and undignified dancing. It's just their honest response to the goodness of God and all that they have experienced in tremendous difficulty.

The Holy Spirit loves to show up when they gather together, and the Father loves their worship. The long hours spent praying for one another and seeking God is not an inconvenience or a distraction from better things, but a hunger that is vital. Several of our friends are children of martyrs, who now have their own families and have launched initiatives in the countries and cities where their parents were killed. Walking with them as friends through the early stage of loss, pain, and questions was not always easy, and Scripture helps us with maturity by instructing us to "Rejoice with those who rejoice, and weep with those who weep" (Romans 12:15). However, the places of deep sobriety are also marked with unusual hope and joy. Crying with someone and laughing with them, sometimes in the space of a few minutes causes a friendship to develop that is not easily broken. Most are beautifully restored, and some of their assignments and ministries are incredible. Joy saturated, love saturated, and fierce. Paul wrote to the church in Corinth:

> *Five times I received from the Jews the forty lashes minus one. Three times I was beaten with rods, once I was pelted with stones, three times I was shipwrecked, I spent a night and a day in the open sea, I have been constantly on the move. I have been in danger from rivers, in danger from bandits, in danger from my fellow Jews, in danger from Gentiles; in danger in the city, in danger in the country, in danger at sea; and in danger from false believers. I have labored and toiled and have often gone*

without sleep; I have known hunger and thirst and have often gone without food; I have been cold and naked. Besides everything else, I face daily the pressure of my concern for all the churches (2 Corinthians 11:24-28 NIV).

Because of love for Jesus, the persecuted Church worldwide is willing to pay a price to see the Kingdom advanced. The God of joy and the joy of God is not an add-on or an option for them, but a *divine necessity*. The kind of joy that emerges even in the middle of profound and potentially devastating loss. The kind of joy that accompanies forgiveness of their enemies who wrong them and hurt loved ones at the deepest levels, sometimes taking their lives in the name of honoring their own god. What kind of joy grows despite all of this? The supernatural kind. The kind that doesn't have its origin with humans.

Consider it pure joy, my brothers and sisters, whenever you face trials of many kinds, because you know that the testing of your faith produces perseverance. Let perseverance finish its work so that you may be mature and complete, not lacking anything (James 1:2-4 NIV).

But rejoice to the extent that you partake of Christ's sufferings, that when His glory is revealed, you may also be glad, with exceeding joy (1 Peter 4:13).

Where the Church that Jesus loves is persecuted, a record is being written in Heaven and the books will be opened[9] at the culmination of history. Within the mystery of God, forgiving those who mistreat us now is giving permission for the God of Justice to extend future vindication and a future reward. I personally believe that the lives of martyrs and the suffering church will be everlasting markers for the reward system of heaven,[10] and their heroic stories will be read as evidence in the court of Heaven. Leaving those who have consistently rejected Jesus without excuse at the end of the age as the multiple accounts of the faithful Church are presented.

The paradox of suffering and joy speaks to the goodness of God, in that He is the Father who provides joy for us in a greater measure than any human agency or demonic force attempt to extinguish. It was the promise of you and I, and all nations, restored to the Father that furnished Jesus with joy as He endured the cross[11]—and it was the reality of God's joy, peace, and presence that empowered Paul to endure shipwreck, famine, riots, beatings, danger, accusations, and imprisonment.[12] I am absolutely convinced that we are not asked to abandon our inheritance of joy to fulfill the will of God. Yes, there are times of extreme difficulty and pain that will seem beyond our ability and capacity to endure—the disciples even write about sensing "the sentence of death"[13]—but nowhere in Scripture do I see God asking or expecting an exchange of our joy, peace, and righteousness in order to walk in what He has for us. It is just not something that He ever asks us to do.

This is a crucial issue to wrestle down, and I pray that it hits hard, and hits deeply. In fact, God wants to increase our capacity to *walk through whatever persecution He asks us to* with deposits of His joy that glorify and speak of Him as His people. Part of our very witness to the world is the fact that we carry joy that is not superficial or transient, but a joy that actually transcends natural capacity. A joy that really shouldn't be present unless something supernatural *was* fueling it. A joy that is not natural, or usual, or typical.

Maybe in our weakness, God's perfect joy will show up and people will see Him and know that it is only because of Him we are different. In the middle of challenges that would normally dissolve joy, we get to live in the immovable and deep-seated joy of the Father who delights in people and overcomes darkness, drinking from a source that is not our own, fueled by a reserve that does not come from us.

• • •

REDISCOVERING JOY: STEP 5

Engage in Prayer

> *Holy Spirit, thank You that You are here 24/7 and have been sent as the Spirit of truth, the Guide, and the Comforter to live with me and in me forever. Thank You for making everything that has been made available from the Father a reality in my life and to those around me. You are the Interface, the Source, the River that Jesus said would flow from my innermost being. My desire is to host you in deeper and more powerful ways, not to use You for something, but to listen, learn, be led, and empowered by You in whatever the Father is doing. Thank You that You are near both in the everyday details, and the miraculous moments. Thank You for Your presence that surrounds my life. I lean into more of You now to walk out a saturated, joy-filled, and resurrection-empowered life.*

Reflection

- Reflect on what it means to cultivate a place of honor in your life for God to be Himself. How can you make room for moments, situations, and interactions where you make room for God to be God, rather than anticipating Him merging with your plans and desires?

- Think through a typical day with all of its demands, schedule, and necessities. How might you respond to the invitation to engage in a new level of awareness of His presence? To answer invitations from Him whenever they might come? What does it look like to be trusted by God?

- Consider if your life has ever been impacted by the adversity of the persecuted Church. What would it cost to follow Jesus in the middle of threats upon your life, or a potential jail sentence for being a follower of Jesus? What does the book of Acts reveal about the dedication and joy of the first-century Church?

Activation

- Take time to soak for an extended time in the presence of God, without an agenda or desired outcome. Make room for God to be Himself around you. Ask Him what He would like to talk about, if anything, and what He would like to reveal to You. Our spirit and our time are two of the most valuable commodities we possess.

Giving Him total access to both is one of the most essential gifts we can give to Him. This is what friendship looks like. Watch joy increase through a deeper connection with the Father.

- Conduct some research on the persecuted Church in a region of the earth. Lend your heart to think about these believers and pray. For further information regarding the work our organization is involved with in the Middle East, contact us to discover ways to partner and become more informed.

6

Joy Blockers

Joylessness is an epidemic, and a challenge we were
created for—provoking and inviting us to contend for the
pure and vibrant joy of God to be experienced and established
in our own lives and in our world. In the opening chapter, we
discussed certain lenses that we can look through in order to
help build a framework to reclaim the joy that is inherent in
God Himself, and now available to us through the power of the
Spirit. We looked at capacity, receiving, and depletion, all important issues in assessing our personal ability to increase in joy.
Second, we discussed lenses that are crucial for a joyful framework—thinking redemptively, transformational perspective, and
anticipating upgrades.

In this chapter, we will look at various hindrances that can
keep us from an increased capacity for joy or cause it to be redi-
rected and stolen from us before we ever get to enjoy it or give
it away. Some of these categories can, of course, influence other
areas of our lives as well as our joy capacity. My hope is to highlight adjustments that we can make to align in a greater way with

the joy that Heaven is releasing, and successfully navigate around factors that block its place and presence in our lives.

Highlighting possibilities to combat and reverse negative influences is extremely useful and spiritual principles help us; however, methods alone cannot replace being intimately led by Holy Spirit. The Spirit of truth by His very nature does not hide truth from us, rather He *will* let us come to the end of ourselves if we insist on it, until we run headlong into truth as a last resort. In my experience, when we come honestly and openly to dialogue with Him, He speaks clearly, and has answers ready and waiting for us.

Read this chapter prayerfully and take your time in dialoguing with God about things that surface for you. My hope is that you will be supernaturally healed of some of the roots behind diminished joy, because God loves to do this. Likewise, He will also reveal developed patterns of behaving, responding, or relating to life that keep you trapped in cycles that lock out or actually *resist* God's joy. These lifestyle patterns have probably developed over time, and the Father is interested in us seeing clearly, learning His ways, and finding keys to the pathway out, so that we don't fall into the same ditch again. He wants to empower us to take responsibility for these patterns of thinking and responding. In this way, we also emerge with wisdom for the next generation and those we mentor.

ADJUSTING HOW WE SEE GOD, OURSELVES, AND OTHERS

How we see God is perhaps the single most important issue in our lives. It determines whether we will run *to Him or from Him,* influences the core of our identity, affects how we see and relate to others, even determining the level of intimacy we will pursue with Him, the level of trust we will place in Him, and the level of transparency and truth we will live in, to name some. Ultimately, how we see God will absolutely determine whether we will relate to and access joy, and to what extent.

Darkness does everything possible to distort and manipulate the image of God so that we will live below the intended level of relationship with Him that He has determined and designed for us. Because of this, we also reflect an incomplete or inaccurate image of Him to the world. However, creating us in His image and restoring us to relationship with Him through Jesus reveals the greatest intentional love. We have heard that He is love so many times, but we should not allow that fact to become rote for us. We will live for a lifetime discovering the depths of who He is, and then into eternity we will continue to joyfully discover incalculably more. Forever.

Insisting on seeing a distorted image of God is like living with a scratch on the lens of our eyesight that affects our perception of everything that we see. We often don't *know* these biases are there, and it may not be our fault that they *are* there. But we are ultimately responsible for allowing them to dictate our view of who He is, how we see ourselves and others, and how we act and respond to life because of it. The invitation then, is to renew our thinking, to embrace many reset moments, and welcome the upgrades that enable us to see Him as He truly is. The Holy Spirit loves to help us with this.

If we see God's primary role in His own story as an angry judge, then we will not only live in unhealthy fear of Him, but also vehemently defend Him in this role, bringing everything we encounter under a judgment paradigm. If we mistakenly believe that *we have earned our own righteousness* before a demanding judge, we will also demand that *everyone else also earn theirs*. The outcome is that we also will become transformed into playing the role of an angry judge. The religious leaders who gathered around Jesus had this paradigm perfected.

Alternatively, seeing God as a buddy who high-fives us while winking at our sin, even when it hurts people, distorts truth, and destroys relationships, will produce unaccountable lives and unleash us as immature people upon an unsuspecting world—convinced that there are zero consequences for our actions and wrongly believing that love irresponsibly disregards the hurt and pain that sin causes. The result is that we will become reckless-wounders in the name of pursuing our own so-called freedom.

I have intentionally highlighted two extremes here. The reality is that most of us do not live in the hypocrisy of either one, but we can unknowingly embrace hybrids of either paradigm, living and acting out of a distorted view of God. I hope that it becomes easy for you to grasp the sad implications of seeing God in only one distorted dimension. The truth is that He is Judge and He is Friend. Jesus was actually both—a friend of sinners. Scripture makes room for Him in both of these roles. He is also *perfect* love, which overarches *everything*. He isn't just loving, He *is* love itself.

In wanting us to receive an accurate perception of who He is, God has revealed Himself in many ways and through many names to His people in the Old and New Testament Scriptures. The ultimate and final revealing was Himself as Father through the representation of Jesus, the Son.

...Anyone who has seen me has seen the Father.

—JESUS (JOHN 14:9 NIV)

God as Father summarizes the whole of history. I like to believe that it's the name He likes best, and the name He left for last. After everything else was revealed—Deliverer, Redeemer, Healer, Self-Sustaining One, Creator, Elohim, Adonai—He determined that the Son would come, and therefore a *Father* would be revealed. The Father of Creation, from whom Jesus and every name on earth derives its name and identity.[1] Knowing God as Father enables us to position correctly as His children. We are saved, we are forgiven, chosen, made righteous—so many incredible truths are outlined about our identity in Christ—but ultimately it is all summed up in *sonship*.

We are all firstborn sons, whether male or female.[2] Pursuing God in His own image as Father causes us to calibrate and healthily position in our roles and identity as children. Seeing Him in His fullest identity, releases us into ours, and empowers us to see others in theirs. Orphan thinking and living becomes disempowered and we no longer have to grasp for position, compete, make our own way, or secure our own future. We are fathered, and others are too; and there is enough room in the house for everyone.

Let's take another moment to stop and connect our hearts with God. This kind of love is available right here, and accessible for you. He is not holding back. Take a moment to receive the love of the Father before you continue. Let it saturate you deeply, and break the power of fear, performance, and insecurity. You are a child of God the Father.

Finally, in adjusting how we see God, Scripture tells us that we become what we worship.[3] The Old Testament command to avoid worshiping idols is less about restriction and more about protection from an image *other than His* being formed in us:

> *But their idols are silver and gold made by human hands, they have mouths but cannot speak, eyes, but cannot see. They have ears, but cannot hear.... Those who make them will be like them and so will all who trust in them* (Psalm 115:4-8 NIV).

If we want to be spiritually deaf, blind, and mute, then worshiping idols is a great kick-starter. Our wonderful God, knowing the spiritual reality that we *become* what we worship, desires only for *His image* to be branded in us, not another alternative, inferior, or distorted image of a pseudo-god. God will answer us according to our idols[4] because His kindness requires that we are never slaves to a lesser God. He will expose our distorted view of Him because His goodness requires that we see Him as He is, and He demands that the world catch a glimpse, not a shadow. A representation, a re-presentation of His true likeness, in us. What a bold, dynamic, joyful, and courageous role we are invited to play. Seeing God as He is and knowing Him as Father is our highest call, so let us pursue seeing God in His own image, and not in one that we have shaped for Him.

Let's stop for a moment and reset, leaning into Holy Spirit who carries all of the wisdom that we need. Ask Him what He wants to speak to you today. I have discovered that He is amazing at knowing how to move us into a moment with Father without overwhelming us, while bringing us into truth and an opportunity for increased capacity and an upgrade. Take a moment to listen.

UNDERSTANDING OUR OWN PERSONAL HISTORY

Some of the places where the greatest joy was stolen from us reveal some of the *greatest places of our authority to release joy for others*. It is true that we get to meet others with empathy in the places we have personally walked through pain. This is valid and beautiful. It is also true that pain and loss is healable, and we are copartners with God to help move others beyond healing into full restoration, in the very same areas where devastation tried to dominate and become a banner of their lives.

Some of the darkest places of your history and some of the weakest places of your flesh reveal some of the greatest places of anointing and redemptive gifting. Of course, a reentry into ministering to arenas of our past failures are to be saturated with wisdom, timing, accountability, and a new approach. However, it remains that some of the greatest struggles reveal some of the greatest redemptive gifts in our lives. If we dare to look carefully—from a new creation perspective, through the Father's lens—we will see.

The experiential knowledge of the realm of the spirit has been evident to me from a young age. Pre-Jesus this was sometimes an interesting and confusing journey. Perceiving, knowing, "picking-up" on everything in a room, a person, or relationship, or situation without having answers or knowing the One who created it all. As part of the gift-mix upon my life, I was hardwired for interaction with and experience of the spiritual world, but in an un-regenerated version of myself, the world was intense, dark, and overwhelming. Encountering God's love through Jesus changed everything. Experiencing His forgiveness, cleansing, and acceptance was amazing in itself.

In addition to all of this, the revelation of how the spiritual realm works and the reordering and renewing of my mind regarding the spiritual reality in which we live was one of the greatest and most liberating gifts from the Father's heart to me. What I had known in shadows and incomplete understanding, as well as from a foundation of fear, I suddenly understood in light, revelation, and from a foundation of love. Carrying Heaven's atmosphere as a believer made total and perfect sense to me, along with the realm of angels, demons, the Holy Spirit, prophecy, feeling, seeing, and knowing things through the person of the Holy Spirit.

As a new believer, I experienced dreams, visions, encounters, and information in many forms from Holy Spirit about the world around me, and it was wonderful. These replaced the shadowed and fearful knowings and sensings I had experienced all of my life outside of Jesus. In my own walk with God, some of the greatest places of fear have become the greatest places of gifting.

Paying attention to our obvious gift-mix, our history, what God has spoken, what others say about us, and where our primary places of favor and opportunity lie help provide a road map for us to understand and steward our destiny and navigate into a redemptive paradigm regarding our future, who we are, and the joy God has created us for.

UPGRADING THE DISCERNING OF SPIRITS, BURDEN BEARING AND EMPATHY

The gift of discerning of spirits (1 Corinthians 12:10) is one of the most misunderstood but powerful gifts given to us by the Holy Spirit. It can function as a powerful upgrade, or alternatively siphon off our life and joy. We can wrongly assume that discerning of spirits has mostly to do with identifying demons and deliverance ministry; and although one of the functions of this gift is accurately discerning darkness, focusing on the demonic just scratches the surface of its purpose.

Being overfocused or overwhelmed by demonic activity is actually a downgrade of this gift and how it operates, and can adversely affect the level of joy that we walk in. Specifically recognizing, discerning, and identifying activity in the spiritual world around us—whether human, angelic, demonic, or the Holy Spirit—is part of what this gift brings to the table. If you have a strong gift of discerning of spirits, or if you do not understand it at all, this should be helpful for you as we discuss this further and how it relates to joy. We will spend some extended time here, because I am discovering that this is a significant issue for many in the Body, and a reason why joy is being stolen from many.

As we have already discussed, what is visible to us was made out of the actually more real and permanent eternal invisible world; but we have a tendency to live in one of two extremes—either fearing the spiritual realm or dismissing it as irrelevant. It's a mistake to avoid the discerning of spirits because it is not easy to understand, or we fear that we are venturing into occult territory. This results in disempowering part of the *advantage* Holy

Spirit intends to give us as the Church. Again, the reality of the spiritual realm was here long before Adam and Eve were created, starting with the Godhead and the plan from eternity past to bring this world we enjoy into existence. As primarily spiritual beings, we are created to be like our Father, who is spirit,[5] and exists in the spiritual realm.

We will not go into extensive expanding of this gift here, but simply speaking, it can be likened to spiritual "intelligence," operating in the realm of perception, knowing and seeing, a powerful diagnostic and information-gathering tool. But even more than this, bringing *Heaven's answers and perspective* to what is identified and real in the invisible is its primary purpose. As with any spiritual gift, functioning within a healthy Church community with pastoral, teaching, evangelistic, prophetic, and apostolic insight and perspective brings context and a framework for the operation of discerning of spirits within the wider Body and to whatever sphere of influence God is giving.

Being healthily connected into a local church body is essential for everyone, but especially for those who operate in this and other revelatory gifts. If you are the most anointed person you know, find a wider sphere of friends and mentors so that your gift can expand within the context of a mature spiritual community.

As a student living in central London, my halls of residence were situated near the financial district. A year into surrendering to Jesus, I was experiencing visions, dreams, and encounters that were beyond anything I had experienced before. Walking in the streets of London, I remember the moment when the gift of discerning of spirits was activated. My spiritual eyes, which

Scripture calls "the eyes of your heart,"[6] were opened and I could "see" what I could not previously see.

During this particular encounter, every person who walked past me on the busy streets had a word "written" on their forehead; some were positive, and some were painful. I could sense a wave of emotion, feelings, and a specific level of intensity that accompanied each word. These stood as headlines over each person's life, and what they were identified by, or the primary atmosphere that was surrounding them. Some were obvious and could be seen in the physical, on their countenance or demeanor, but some were not. Some were individuals who looked extremely put together who had learned to mask pain, and some were those the London business district would disregard for looking "less than," but who carried great treasure.

I share this with you to highlight a moment that clarified things for me. The compassion and wonder of God was resting upon me as I experienced this, and the aim for that moment was not to judge, fix, or communicate—it was simply an exercise in *knowing*. I did not have time to speak to every person or share what I was receiving, but I had been drafted into a training exercise that God had initiated. We could technically say that I was experiencing a combination of discerning of spirits, a seer gift, and the word of knowledge.

As a worship leader for many years and now a mentor, one of the primary giftings worship leaders are to carry is the discerning of spirits—monitoring the human realm in the room, the angelic and demonic realm, and most importantly, tracking with the journey that the Holy Spirit wants to take us on in worship. Knowing when a different facet of God's presence has entered the room or identifying a transitioning to what He is doing next is crucial.

So, what does all of this have to do with joy? We have deliberately spent time expanding some facets of discerning of spirits because those who operate in this space often deal with tremendous spiritual weight and emotional interference that can hijack and massively affect their joy level, often causing physiological responses in the body. Maybe this description resonates with you personally. Or maybe, it is time to understand someone close to you or in your church on a heightened level. Some like to use the terminology "burden bearing" or "empathy," and in the marketplace we talk in terms of emotional intelligence, all of which can certainly describe some of the functions and release of discerning of spirits. God is informing us and overlaying wisdom onto the powerful operation of our gifts in order for us to no longer be sidetracked or defeated, but fully empowered to jump over distractions and the misappropriation of our gifts, seeing them *fully* redeemed and joyfully functioning for the advancement of the Kingdom.

Some people with a prophetic, or discerning of spirits gift often see the world differently, and at times can relate to heavenly realities much more significantly than earthly realities. Their priority is weighted on what is happening in the spiritual world, rather than how to win people for Christ or teaching exegetically through a New Testament epistle. This doesn't stop them from leading people to Christ or negate God from using them to lead a Bible study, it is just not their primary gift. Their sensitivity level is often high as they navigate sensing changes geographically, emotionally, circumstantially, or atmospherically.

What the average person perceives at a "level ten" in intensity, can feel like a "level one hundred" to feelers and discerners. This is especially true if we are still wounded, have not sufficiently learned how our gift works, or how to turn it off when appropriate. In times of national or international crisis, this is intensified further as we diagnose the pervading atmosphere, which is at times turbulent. Our way forward then is to be mentored, trained, healed, and connected healthily into a church body where we can both give and receive life, so that our gift emerges in the context of a complete perspective of the Kingdom. We then grow in relational and personal maturity, in community with a diverse and mature body of believers.

Relational health has been one of the greatest areas of personal development during my journey with Jesus, and there is still room to expand! My wife, Shirin, is particularly strong in this area and has taught and imparted wisdom to me. Early on in our relationship she would confront me when I was unknowingly operating in unhealthy ways of relating. Most were literal blind spots for me—areas I had no idea about and no perception of the potential hurt I could cause others. The good news is, my skills are still expanding, and now much more developed than they were two decades ago.

Two international trips several years apart illustrate God's healing intent toward me and the discerning of spirits and prophetic gifts on my life. Traveling internationally multiple times a year has been part of my routine for a couple of decades, and I consider it an honor to connect with diverse cultures and the Body of Christ to help equip and build.

During an extended trip to Asia, we connected with several churches and ministries in different regions. In one particular city, intimidation and fear was manifesting itself in an unusual way. My internal radar was aware of registering constant spiritual threats, and as soon as I prayed and backed it off, which would normally take care of such opposition, it would reform again. Resting in God, worshiping, declaring Scripture, ignoring it, and commanding it to go was not working. The eighteen-hour day ministry schedule was intense, and to say that I was being tormented is an understatement.

I intentionally reviewed an internal checklist: I had prayed over the hotel room; knew that God had sent me; determined if I was simply overtired; confirmed that the invitation was approved by the US apostolic team I am part of; checked in with our team of intercessors; researched the host ministry and what they carry; and of course, personally prayed to hear from Jesus. All of this was in place.

Not everything we encounter is "warfare" related when traveling internationally, some things are natural dynamics that we learn to manage and counteract in healthy ways. However, the level of intimidation I was experiencing on this trip was unreasonable, unyielding, and persistent. This did not result in joy or peace and was a distraction to much of what He wanted me to see and release. The gift of discerning of spirits that was meant to be a blessing to the Body of Christ was actually *working against me* in this situation. This may be a reality for you in your everyday life. I realized that I was clearly living below the Father's highest and best for me.

After arriving home and talking with some mature friends, I realized that the Lord had exposed a vulnerability *in me* that He wanted to heal. I had experienced the love of the Father and knew that His perfect love neutralizes and cancels fear, but there were still places in my soul that were not responding to God but reacting to darkness.

After receiving ministry and cleaning out generational iniquity and trauma in my history, something shifted. The travel experience was not just something that I was supposed to "faith" or declare my way out of; instead, the Father wanted to unravel and showcase the components and process that had led me to the place of vulnerability. It was time to confront an area of darkness, a landing place for fear and intimidation in my life, so it had no access in the future. I now travel worldwide without fear and intimidation—even through experiencing bomb threats, volcanic ash clouds, emergency plane landings, and assignments in countries where the church is forbidden to meet.

Several years a later, a second experience highlights a significant difference. Flying into Dubai, my wife and I were taking advantage of a one-night layover before continuing on to another country. As the plane began to land, I experienced wave after wave of spiritual information as I picked up on the pervading atmosphere in the city, including downloads regarding key areas of darkness, strengths, redemptive gifts of the region, God's strategies, angelic presence, and an overall "sense" of the atmosphere. The Holy Spirit suddenly asked me, "What are you doing?" I answered that I was receiving strategy for my assignment here. There was a pause, and He graciously informed me to "Stop and relax," explaining that He already had people in place and wanted me to simply enjoy the city and be refreshed before heading on. I laughed as this was simply the *heart of the Father* for me in that moment.

Of course, we are always ready to respond to what God asks of us; but in this instance, not only was I no longer tormented by the darkness that I perceived, I was free to follow the Father who was *telling me to rest*. Steady in His love, not as a slave but a son. I wanted to argue that there were people who needed Jesus, and there were things to pray, and strategies to extract, but this was not my assignment.

Two trips separated by several years and significant healing. Two different hearts, and two different responses. Now I am often aware of angelic presence that accompany me as I land in countries, that remain with me for the entire visit. The Father was generous to highlight an area He wanted to strengthen that was stealing and robbing my joy. He orchestrated the perfect moment to address it so I could hold the ground and move forward unhindered, sensing Him *above* everything. He's just that good.

I am not implying that every place of intense warfare we encounter will require inner healing, as there are many situations that require us to simply stand.[7] However, in the context of a gift of discerning of spirits, it is important to understand the place for healing and restoration so that our joy is not repeatedly stolen.

Some application as we move forward:

1. Allow Jesus to fully heal and restore our souls. Although we do not live by feelings, a gift of discerning of spirits needs the *full bandwidth of healed emotions*. Jesus died for the redemption of

our emotions, not the nullifying of them. We often quote that He is the restorer of our souls,[8] without actually embracing the fullness of what that means for us. We are to no longer limp through life distracted by fear and intimidation from the realm of the spirit; our souls (mind, will, and emotions) can be fully healed to be conduits of Him and His purpose.

2. Correctly measure your sphere of influence and authority. In picking up spiritual information, we can sometimes unknowingly interfere in spheres where we have not been given authority or been called by God. Because my personal sphere of influence includes closed countries in Middle East that has grown over several years, this indicates a sphere or *metron* that I am responsible for. When I am "picking up" something, I have to ask Holy Spirit, "What specifically is this related to? Individual, family, neighborhood, local church, city, nation, Middle East? What sphere of my influence does this relate to? What do You want me to do with it, if anything?"

3. Turn off unwanted information. At times we need to turn off our gift and *simply stop picking up unwanted information*. Acknowledging and absorbing everything you feel will steal your joy. Turn it off.

4. Offload. Know when you are overwhelmed through burden bearing. Scripture does instruct

us to carry each other's burdens[9]—but not to be overwhelmed by them. There are times that I spend extended time with Jesus, handing over every specific detail of what is a weight to me. Scripture tells us to ***cast our burdens onto Jesus***. This is a violent word. We come to the Cross and can cast every burden onto the blood and power of the greatest sacrifice of all history.

5. **Check unforgiveness and anger at the door.** The cost of remaining in unforgiveness or anger is too high for anyone, but especially those who operate in discerning of spirits. It nullifies clarity and disables effectiveness toward those we are in anger toward. It significantly shuts down our gift.

6. Know when we are just tired. Sometimes we need to acknowledge that we are simply **tired or navigating unusual stress** in our sphere of operation. Realizing if a lack of sleep or need for rest is influencing us negatively helps us to stop and recuperate.

HEALING FROM WOUNDS AND TRAUMA

Sometimes areas in our lives that are still unhealed can be the cause of diminished joy. Some of our issues come from thinking incorrectly, which we will talk about next. But, sometimes, we have bruises and wounds in our soul or spirit, just like those we experience in our physical body. They are unseen with the natural eye, but the evidence of their existence manifests in our responses, emotions, or behavior. Similar to a bruise on the skin that is painful to the touch, bruises on our soul cause pain when something provokes or brushes that area. If viewed correctly, pain is actually a friend, as it informs us of places that require much-needed attention. A significant level of transformation happens to us when we are born again, and many bondages and wounds are immediately healed as a result of coming to Christ.

However, experience reveals that there are some areas of our lives that are not instantly healed or resolved, and the process of discipleship brings order and change. In other instances, we need to appropriate the finished work of Jesus and receive healing in our soul and spirit. These may be the result of *things done to us* such as abuse, or *not done* such as severe neglect. There are also generational wounds or rebellion to consider, carried in the family line, manifesting in different ways in different generations, and there may also be demonic activity involved that may be empowering the issue.

The great news is that God has already made provision for our healing and restoration. At times, He will heal us in stages so that we are able to hold on to our healing, gain wisdom as to what got us there in the first place, and learn how to remain free. Inner healing is as profound and life altering as a physical healing—and making room for it in our lives is wisdom. I personally believe that it is an absolute necessity for every Christian. Wounds and trauma from our past can siphon joy from our everyday lives, and the price that Jesus paid for our complete restoration is more than enough to restore and heal us from the inside out.

There are several powerful inner healing or ministry models addressing and bringing freedom, which are listed in the resource section at the back of the book.[10]

PAUSING NEGATIVE THOUGHTS

Negative thinking can be focused on the past, present, or future, debilitating us from either perspective. It is not difficult to grasp that there is an abundance of negativity easily discoverable in our past, in the current cultural narrative, or that manifests as anxiety regarding what might or might not happen in our future. If we do not learn to pause the influx, it can overwhelm us and definitely shut off and restrict opportunities for joy.

Because negative self-talk is a personal landing place for other toxic mindsets, it is a fantastic starting place for us to consider. We thrive when we agree with who God says that we are in Christ,[11] and any thought that we entertain that does not line up with this reality will create for us an inferior reality and unhealthy thought life. Negative self-talk can manifest in many ways, centering on our appearance, ability, perceived success, identity, level of hope and manifesting in shame, hopelessness, rejection, and discouragement, etc. These are partly the fruit of thoughts that do not align with what the Bible says about our new identity as children of God. He wants to *replace these hopeless thoughts with His thoughts* in regard to how He sees us, and what He has done to reposition us.

We absolutely needed a Savior. We are not worthy—but He is. And He has changed our name and our identity forever. Negative thoughts must be stripped of their authority to talk us out of our worthiness to live in abundant peace and joy. We can rest in the fact that we are *not* worthy to earn our own righteousness—but He was. We are absolutely treasured. And now the ultimate Joy Giver lives in us.

Catching every thought that does not line up with what your Father says about you and taking it captive[12] will *leave room in your thought life for the thoughts that God has toward you, and others, and every sphere you are created to have influence.*

Anxiety and worry, along with other negative thoughts, are manifestations of fear, and are prevalent in communication from the media, social media, and even in the atmosphere. Living meditating on anxious thoughts or worry instead of Him will absolutely diminish our joy. Paralyzing anxiety and worry are often future focused and rely on negative scenarios, "what if" possibilities, and potential outcomes. This is actually the fruit of misdirected hope—faith in the wrong direction. Unfortunately, living in a worried and anxious state can cause us to arrive at a place where we eventually have *more faith for the negative, than in God's promises.* We can also wrongly believe that our high level of anxiety and fear is normal, when our capacity is actually absolutely full. This can cause us to overflow regularly, overwhelmed with fear and anxiety, and leaves us no room for unexpected circumstances that may place a demand on our hope and faith.

Living in the past through regret, condemnation, guilt, and disappointment are negative thought patterns focused on what has already happened. There is nothing we can do to change what did or did not happen to us. But we can be healed of the pain and unforgiveness associated with our history.

In the arena of negative thinking, some powerful answers are to: mediate on what God says about us in His Word, allow His perfect love to break the power of fear (perfect love casts out fear[13] and low reserves of love causes fear to increase), live in awareness that not every thought we have originates with us, and practice replacing whatever thoughts do not line up with Scripture. These are lifestyle patterns for a lifetime of joy.

NAVIGATING DEMONIC ACTIVITY

Some of the resistance we encounter to joy in our lives can be attributed to demonic activity. The two primary ways that this happens is through invitation or intrusion—what we invite into our lives through actions that are contrary to God's Word and ways, and what intrudes or invades in an attempt to oppress us. The father of lies comes to steal, kill, and destroy; and therefore, the restoration of joy will often be contested in our lives. However, the really good news is that Jesus came to give us life in abundance,[14] is totally victorious, and is living inside us by His Spirit, carrying powerful solutions for every circumstance.

In completely disarming[15] the authority of the forces of darkness through the cross and resurrection, Jesus settled forever the issue of His preeminence and ensured that they are forever subject to His name. Every demonic entity, from low-level demons to principalities over regions are absolutely and totally aware of His name and reign. The question remains, though, are *we* absolutely and totally aware? Believing a lie or not being aware of the truth are two major reasons why we can be in bondage and not realize it. We need each other and we need the Body of Christ to help us see what we do not see by ourselves.

Repenting of decisions, actions, and behavior that are contrary to His Word and ways is a great place for us to start in stopping the invitation cycle to any demonic activity. We cannot exercise authority over what we give a deliberate landing place for in our lives.[16] We are not talking about religious faultlessness here, which demands perfection of ourselves or others to earn righteousness. We are also not referring to our already secured position in Christ. We are addressing *removing a landing place* for what comes to steal from us and attempts to take the greater portion of our peace, hope, strength, and joy.

In specific relationship to reclaiming joy, three primary spirits to be watchful for are a spirit of heaviness, the religious spirit, and a spirit of slumber. If God promises to give us praise for a spirit of heaviness, it stands to reason that heaviness will assign itself against the release of joy. A religious spirit, as has been said, will attempt to place unreasonable demands and performance upon us to cause us to attempt to deliver what only God can produce—righteousness, perfection, and the fruit of the Spirit. A spirit of slumber, although similar to heaviness, is manifest particularly in inactivity and procrastination, inoculating us against stepping into all that God has for us.

As we have discussed, it is my experience that engaging with personal ministry and inner healing can disarm and remove roots that empower or give place to demonic activity. Jesus has paid the ultimate price for us to be totally free.[17]

CULTIVATING A HEALTHY VIEW
OF THE END TIMES

The issue of the "end times" stirs extremely strong viewpoints, emotional reactions, and responses within different streams of the Body of Christ. This is not the place for an extended presentation or debate on the validity of various end-time positions or doctrine. Nor is it my desire to convince you of the supremacy of one position over another; there are many people whom I love and respect and am in relationship with, whose views sit on various places along the end-times spectrum. However, my observation is that certain perspectives provide greater opportunity to lean out of the joy that God intends for us.

Our eschatological, or end-time, view matters because it actually determines what we focus on and often the extent to which we will engage our world, or simply wait for an escape. Whether we believe the world and its systems are *able to be transformed or are beyond help* will determine whether we as Christians reverse out of opportunities in politics, business, cultural debate, higher education, academia, scientific research, etc., or engage as an influence and representative of Heaven. These are two opposite extremes, but will hopefully help us to quickly identify the issue at hand.

Theologically speaking, Classical Pentecostalism (emerging at the beginning of the 20th century) became connected to a particular view of the end times called premillennial dispensationalism. Simply put, this framed the whole of history into specific time periods, or dispensations, and presented the end times through the lens that everything would become increasingly harrowing,[18] and culminate in the sudden and secret rapture of the Church, leaving the "lost" to be left behind, suffering a dreadful tribulation. This view resulted in the Church's disengagement over several decades with the world's systems and structures, which could "not be redeemed," but would be destroyed. Along with this, an increased intrigue with "reading the times," and attempts at predicting dates for the return of Jesus and the rapture of the Church based on literal events dominated the attention of certain sectors of the Body of Christ.

It is important to note that this has not always been the dominant end-time view of the Church in previous centuries. The great cathedrals, hospitals, social justice movements, and societal institutions were born out of a biblical worldview that the Church was to influence and serve culture and the world to bring transformation. Their focus was less upon escaping the planet, and more upon transforming it for the generations to come. It is also interesting to note that an extreme dispensational view of end times does not translate very well into cultures outside of the United States, particularly those where Christians are already suffering persecution and death for their faith. For them, the "tribulation" has already happened, and they live daily in the paradox of the challenge of the Kingdom "now and not yet" as did the early New Testament Church.

Jesus' parable of the weeds shared in Matthew 13, provides wonderful insight for us.[19] Jesus explains that in fact, two crops will *grow up together until the end*—those planted by our Father, and those planted by the enemy. The parable specifically explains that *evil will not be taken out of the harvest field until the very end, and so we can anticipate a maturing of both crops*. It is up to us to determine which crop we will focus on with the time, giftings, and resources we have been given to steward.

In terms of embracing a more victorious eschatology, we are not talking about selfishly preserving our personal joy by ignoring difficulty and injustice in our world; in fact, a victorious Kingdom paradigm results in the exact opposite, because the transformation of individuals and systems is seen as a possibility. Looking through the lens of the whole counsel of God, there is an unmistakable thread of joy, overcoming, and transformation in the meta-narrative of God's story. The issue is *how much of our focus will be dedicated* to the end-times narrative, conspiracy theories, and what darkness is doing. We can find ourselves obsessing over the negative subplot, instead of the glorious fact that good wins in the end. Some are overfocused on issues that we cannot change and have no way of influencing, instead of engaging what the Holy Spirit is asking us to do to bring transformation to the sphere of favor that we do have.

When Jesus states that no one knows the day and time of His return,[20] and instructs us to not worry about tomorrow because each day has enough trouble of its own,[21] He was helping us. When He talked about watching and being prepared, it was always an encouragement to stay connected to Him.[22] There is so much that Jesus has already commissioned us to do that we are not fulfilling. An unhealthy focus upon the end times can exasperate this further, stealing our joy, wrapping us in fear, and causing us to reverse out of the very places Jesus has designed for us to engage.

CLEANING OUT HABITUAL SIN

There are many incredible resources and discipleship material on the issue of getting free from sin patterns that hinder us. The best resources focus upon aligning us with our new nature, rather than rules of behavior modification that don't necessarily tend to the root of our problems. Sin habits are *typically fruit of a deeper root*, and the journey from *temptation to action* is often provoked and led by challenging circumstances, unbelief, stress, difficulty, or rebellion that can cause us to step back into familiar, temporary fixes that ultimately bring destruction to us. Sin is not our friend and it will certainly starve out the joy of the Holy Spirit in our lives.

The lust of the flesh, the lust of the eyes, and the pride of life[23] are realities that do pull on us, but the decision to step out of the boundaries that God says are best for us, is a process that starts with a thought and grows into a desire in our hearts, long before it ever becomes an action.[24] In one sense, we never "accidently fall" into sin; in fact, we run through many stop signs beforehand. Again, allowing God to heal us of any places where we are vulnerable through trauma, wounding, or abuse in our past is a key. Also learning new boundaries and patterns of relating to ourselves and others provides the tools we need to navigate temptation and potential pitfalls.

Ultimately, knowing how much we are unconditionally loved, who we truly are in Him, and who He has created us to be, releases a *mark of dignity and value upon us* that creates a desire to reject anything that will hinder the relationship we have with

Him. Love will drive us toward Him and away from sin; anything that threatens our relationship.

DEALING WITH OFFENSES AND UNFORGIVENESS, JUDGMENTS AND INNER VOWS

It is not difficult to know when we are dealing with an offense, unforgiveness, a judgment, or inner vow. The narrative of our own heart will reveal what is evident and hidden to the natural eye. Because it is true that "out of the abundance of the heart" the mouth speaks,"[25] we can easily hear fruit of an offense or judgment in our own conversation, or in the words that run through our minds. How we respond to the mention of someone's name or a particular incident that happened is also a clue to whether we have forgiven or responded in an unhealthy way to something that has happened to us.

An offense is something that we receive based on something that happened or did not happen in a relational context. We have to first assess our expectations to see if they are realistic, or something we have projected onto the person with whom we have an offense. If we have experienced a legitimate wrong, we have a choice to as to whether *we will receive the offense,* and then a second choice as to whether we will *forgive or hold on to* the offense. It is also possible to take on a third-party offense based on someone else's account of a wrong done to them. This is a massive trap and needs to be avoided, because the offense can linger for us long after the "offended friend" has already forgiven their enemy.

Holding on to unforgiveness hurts us far more than the person who we are offended with and can be described as *drinking poison and expecting someone else to suffer.* Jesus clearly addresses unforgiveness on a number of occasions, including what is historically called the "Lord's Prayer" in Luke 11. The clue is in the phrase "And forgive us our sins, for we also forgive everyone who is indebted to us…" (Luke 11:4). Jesus drops this phrase in the middle of this lifestyle prayer to let us know that *forgiving others is a lifestyle and expected, just as we expect to be forgiven.*

At times we hold others to higher standards than we hold ourselves and will not forgive and release people for wrongs that are small compared to our own faults. Forgiving someone is not agreeing that what they did to you is right, and it is also not entering back into a trusted relationship with them—it is releasing them and therefore freeing yourself from the offense and the pain.

Judgments are similar, but instead attribute a heart motive to something that has been done or said, when truly we cannot know the inner state of another person's heart. A judgment locks someone else into a role or image, usually a negative one, that we then use to look at them or their behavior. Scripture is clear that we are not to judge if we do not want to be judged ourselves.[26] Sometimes a cycle of experiencing judgment from others could be because we have sown a great deal of judgment toward others previously. An inner-vow deals with the issue of our own heart in response to wrong or perceived wrong being done to us. We vow never to repeat the same behavior, or that we will never be like a certain person. This form of stubborn judgment, however justified it may be, causes a root issue that often locks us into the same behavior as those we have judged.

The assignment of a wound or offense is to steal our joy, and to ultimately propel us to become a wounder ourselves. Someone who will perpetuate hurt in others and be the source of stealing joy in other people's lives. When we are bound up with critical thoughts, emotions, and memories about someone or something they did to us, we have little room for God's thoughts. Can joy and peace live alongside a complaining, bitter, and critical spirit? Is there room for the beauty of God's goodness to do its work in and through us?[27]

It is crucial for us to take responsibility to forgive and release others, breaking our agreements with offense and refusing to receive offenses that come our way. In this way, we actually receive authority over the places where we were wronged and can carry anointings and authority in the very areas that came to damage us. We have to ask if holding on to an offense is worth the authority that we will give up in doing so.

ELIMINATING MISCONCEPTIONS ABOUT JOY

We can knowingly or unknowingly live with misconceptions about joy. These can sometimes cloud our expectation or faith for more joy, sometimes circumventing the possibility of holding on to more and cultivating it in our lives.

Much of the Church can seemingly live with making little room for joy in their own lives or the lives of those around them, even celebrating the absence of joy. This is interesting because in Scripture, the absence of joy is often a sign of judgment:

And gladness is taken away, and joy out of the plentiful field; and in the vineyards there shall be no singing, neither shall there be shouting: the treaders shall tread out no wine in their presses; I have made their vintage shouting to cease (Isaiah 16:10 KJV).

Because we are made for joy, and it is an inherent part of our created design, we will look for it and attempt to cultivate it anywhere we can. Like anything else that is ultimately found in Him, when we do not allow Him to satisfy a created need, then we will find inferior substitutes—artificial sweeteners to temporarily lift us out of the lack. This is a sad response when the Father has made room for a permanent, constant, powerful supply of joy to be made available to us from His reserves. Equally, the Church has not always cultivated and modeled the places of joy that are found in God. We have talked about it, included it in our creeds, printed bookmarks with reminders, but have not always demonstrated or lived it out.

Again, please do not hear what I'm not saying. I understand that life in God is not lived from one mountaintop of laughter to the next, and that extremely difficult things happen to us, and to those we love. I am also deeply committed to the Church and value every single local expression of it around the globe. But I wonder, in the West in particular, if we haven't starved our people of celebration, exuberance, and laughter because of some misconceptions about joy and its place in the Kingdom.

Ancient Israel embraced a feast cycle initiated by God. Under that covenant, alongside the sober sacrificial rituals that were necessary for the covering of sin, there were extended community feasts and celebrations that existed to remember God's goodness, deliverance, and love toward them—where they actually experienced joy, hope, refreshing, and laughter within community.[28]

Have you considered that lost people might gravitate toward bars, clubs, and substances because they are starving for joy and connection, and they may not be able to find what they are looking for among the people who call themselves the Church? I am not endorsing those choices, but this may be a greater indictment upon local churches than upon those who don't know Him yet and are running after inferior substitutes.

Another misconception about joy is considering it as fleshly or less spiritual than other expressions. We need to ask if there is room for healthy celebration in our lives that isn't connected to a "spiritual" activity? Could this form of dualism be a reason why the unchurched cannot sometimes relate to our preaching at them, when our lives may not offer a joyful alternative.

We were exploring college options with our eldest son, and a solid, conservative, amazing Christian private school included corporate worship during the student orientation. It was Jesus centered with contemporary songs and a traditional hymn, and attempted to gather strangers together across different denominations, which is always an interesting experiment in itself as I've discovered many times. It would be fair to say that some were less excited about corporate worship than others, but it was a reflective, calm, thought-provoking, and peace-filled time. As the service finished, current students broke into a planned moment where they rushed the stage—a hip-hop track blasted into the auditorium, and a vibrant celebration happened along with cheers from students and parents.

It was a fun moment, but I was also deeply struck by the irony of these two contrasting moments. As nice and sincere as it had been, there had simply not been room for joy in the corporate worship time. It took a "secular" dance track and a stage performance to invite us into shouts that would have been inappropriate in the worship setting a few minutes before. As sad as it is for us not to find joy in every facet of life outside of a church setting, we have equally settled for spiritual settings that do not have room for explosions of joy in response to who God is.

We have talked about the lie that considers joy and loud volume to be less reverent than silence and seriousness. It is so easy for us to relegate joy to a lower level of spirituality in our thinking, or even leave it out of spiritual moments completely. Or even unknowingly allocate joy in different forms to a fleshly, carnal, or soulish category. Joy can of course be rooted in any one of these things, but so also can prayer, evangelism, preaching, and prophecy, along with other things we consider truly spiritual. Come to think of it, being insincerely nice to someone whom we hate in our hearts is soulish at best, and murder at worse. But it can look really spiritual on the outside if you don't have to wrestle down the true heart condition behind the smile.

It's important that we intentionally make room for more joy in our walk with God, receiving it as an aspect of who He is, and a dimension of His Kingdom that reflects and demonstrates this. God is into joy much more than we give Him credit for. What would it look like for culture to rediscover and reclaim multifaceted joy in its practices and creativity? The Christianization of much of the world by the West, in its honorable zeal to clean out paganism, imprinted a version of Western religious systems upon the redemptive gifts and created beauty inbuilt into tribal and regional people groups—often at the expense of creative, prophetic, colorful, and visionary gifts that these bring to the Body of Christ. One of the Middle Eastern networks we have worked alongside for twenty-five years has included celebration as one of their top ten core values as an organization. Now that's joyful!

Another way we can dishonor the place of joy is considering it immature, or maybe *less mature* than other fruit of the Spirit. We can unintentionally elevate patience, peace, and kindness in Christian culture above joy, life, and exuberance. We are in fact in need of it all. We get to make room for the louder laugh, the love of life, and the spontaneous joy that Father loves to bring. It would be a mistake for us to assume that expressions of joy that do not fit all of our boxes as immature in some way.

Genuine joy has often rescued many of us from awkward, difficult, and sometimes boring situations. I am so thankful for people in my sphere who have gifts of joy that they bring to every occasion. Those who are healthy enough not to use it as an attention getter or a dominating distraction, but inject something crucial into our world that is *not less than or more immature than seriousness*—lifting us out of places of zero joy. Anyone who orbits my world for any length of time will realize that I'm quite an intense person, but I also love to laugh. Jesus did not fit into religious boxes. It would be helpful for us not place joy in religious boxes either.

We may not communicate it in this way, but there is also a sense that we sometimes consider joy as shallow or less deep than more important spiritual pursuits. We may mistakenly elevate intellectual or strategic-level thinking above emotive, gut-level feelings or emotions, when they are simply two different functions of a healthy whole. High-level, strategic thinking is absolutely crucial, and I value those who bring this element to our team. However, we are making more room for and quantifying emotional intelligence in culture and the marketplace than ever before, and this is a significant move forward.

Joy encounters with God have sometimes been the places where I have received the greatest clarity regarding future initiatives that have produced massive Kingdom fruit and life. This did not come as a result of an intentional strategy session. Does God only bring strategy through intellectual brainstorming sessions? Or should we neglect all strategic planning because God gives us revelation during a joy encounter? Definitely not. However, we are making room for joy in this exploration, and our tendency in the Western church has been to unknowingly "dis-promote" joy to an inferior delivery system and therefore place it lower on the hierarchy of spiritual reality or disciplines.

Another misconception is that joy can be wrongly attributed to being wasteful or frivolous. The overriding sense being that as long as we are enjoying joy, then we must be missing doing something *more important*. This approach makes experiencing joy seem irresponsible rather than an attribute of God Himself and part of the response mechanism He has inbuilt into creation. Tax collectors, sinners, drunkards, and others whom Jesus was accused of being friends with[29] were occupied having their own version of fun, and Jesus interfaced with them. It is dangerous to say, but maybe in some aspects of their laughter and community, they were living in closer proximity to the joy of Heaven than the religious? Maybe they had discovered aspects of joy that

Jesus recognized, reflecting more of the Father's joyful community than some of the piously religious, and were in fact ready to be introduced to true joy by the Son of laughter.

We have covered significant ground in this chapter that I hope will be useful for you in navigating what comes to block or diminish joy in your life. Stay connected as we explore the science of joy and what research has discovered regarding how we are actually hardwired for laughter and bliss.

• • •

REDISCOVERING JOY: STEP 6

Engage in Prayer

> *Father, I am excited about Your intended pathway to greater deposits and expressions of joy. Today, I choose to say yes to the unraveling of anything that is blocking Your joy from moving in my life. Anything known or unknown, hidden or visible. Thank You for revealing the way forward as You always do when we ask. I acknowledge that You love me too much to live in a place of diminished joy, and so I thank You for a spirit of wisdom and revelation in the knowledge of You, that the eyes of my understanding might be opened (Ephesians 1:17). Uproot and remove anything that is blocking the fullness of joy You have made provision for. I surrender body, soul, mind, and spirit to You and say yes to the invitation to be everything You have created and formed me to be.*

The best version of myself. Joy filled and reflecting Your image in every way.

Reflection

- Give thought to how you primarily "see" God. Do you perceive Him as an angry judge? Disappointed in you? Distant? Unavailable? Indifferent? Or unreachable, or reluctant? Or do you see Him as generous, abundant, and delighting in you? Patient, kind, and good toward you and others? We can at times project the image of our earthly father onto God. Take some time to pray about whether this is the case for you, and what the Father wants to reveal about Himself to adjust this.

- Consider which areas covered in the chapter caught your attention. Assess whether an unhealthy overfocus on the end times, offenses, burden bearing, past wounds, or even misconceptions about joy have contributed to blocking what God wants to do in restoring fullness of joy in your everyday life. Take time to repent and reverse out of ways in which you may have sabotaged yourself and resist the ways in which your enemy has attempted to steal from you. God wants you to recover all.

Activation

- Plan to schedule time for a personal ministry or inner-healing session. Just as important as looking after our physical body, watching over and paying attention to our soul and spirit is vital. There are recommended ministries referenced in the back of the book that can help you receive impacting ministry. Your own church leadership or mentors may also know of mature and reliable ministers who are gifted and anointed to bring freedom and breakthrough.

- After identifying some of the possible pitfalls hindering you, take time to brainstorm the God attributes you are called to carry instead. List the positive opposites to your weak areas and begin to press into Heaven to receive and carry Heaven's answers to the joy blockers for your own life and others.

7

The Science of Joy

*I*n researching the subject of joy in a broad sense, it is interesting to discover that scientific research and particularly brain science is at the forefront of contemporary discussion. Scientific discovery often affirms the Father's design for us, and is increasingly supporting and confirming what has been preserved and written for us in Scripture for thousands of years. Scientific research at its best is simply proving God's Word and His ways to be true. In this chapter we explore some complementary scientific findings that highlight and bring to the forefront what God's people have actually known and practiced for centuries.

Wisdom helps us delve into scientific discovery through the lens of God's Word and ways, not to naively absorb and be led by every trend or to bow to it as a god, but to find *Him reflected* in creation architecture as the Originator of all intelligent design found in the universe. Secularists, science, and research can even at times seemingly "prophesy" to the church, calling us to return and reclaim certain God truths that we ourselves have neglected. This enables us to awake and respond.

Let's take a moment to look at some eye-opening research that will strengthen the reality for you that we are without doubt made in the image of God, who is the most joyful being who has ever, or will ever exist, and therefore created *from* joy and *for* joy.

First, I want to make a distinction between joy and happiness and expand upon an earlier statement, that *God is not obligated to our happiness but has made absolute provision for our joy.* It is not my purpose here to reach definitions and demand that everyone adhere to them, but to help build a framework of communication to support what is on the heart of God for us. For Christians, it appears that joy, both scripturally and experientially, describes a much deeper and permanent state, than simply happiness, which in the eyes of culture often fluctuates according to circumstances.

Are you happy? Do you have joy? Two questions that probe into two very different places. Happiness for the most part is often measured by outward scenarios and speaks to the temperature of how well things are going in our lives; whereas joy delves deeper, asking us to assess what is resident inside and evaluate something much more long term.

In the United States, the "pursuit of happiness" appears front and center in the Declaration of Independence, one of the foundational documents both defining and upholding the ethos of what it means to be American:

> We hold these truths to be self-evident, that all men are created equal, that they are endowed by their Creator with certain unalienable Rights, that among these are Life, Liberty, and the pursuit of Happiness.
> —Declaration of Independence, 1776

Upheld here as one of the unalienable rights of every human being, happiness is celebrated as a vital and divinely given right, placed within our grasp to pursue. The term "we hold these truths to be self-evident," is magnificent to me because it reflects and reinforces a biblical worldview— that inbuilt into creation itself is the obvious, self-evident reality that God has endowed us with rights that come solely from Him. The words "life, liberty, and the pursuit of happiness" were carefully chosen by the writers to champion the importance and value of these God-given rights in the life of *every* human being, and for which governments are created to protect.

It is important to recognize that although not perfect people, Thomas Jefferson and colleagues at the time of writing, were undoubtedly imagining something more comprehensive than personal, private happiness—something more revolutionary than individual joy. Drawing from a Judeo-Christian vantage point, and thinkers such as Aristotle who believed that individual life finds its ultimate meaning in relation to others, the Founders envisioned a preferable future where unalienable, God-given truths were promoted, protected, and pioneered for an entire nation, and for the generations to come.[1]

According to the World Happiness Report, in 2019 the United States ranked 19th on the list of the happiest places in the world.[2] If asked to determine what makes a population is happy, we would probably conclude that financial prosperity and high standards of living were the greatest indicators. But according to global statistics from the last decade; wealth, health, and peace are not the only determining factors in whether populations consider themselves happy.[3]

Although growing up in a country ravaged by war, 80 percent of Somalian youth profess to be happy; and Panama reports one of the highest levels of happiness in South America even though almost one third of the population live below the poverty line. Likewise, decades of violent crime and civil war in Guatemala does not deter its people from being some of the happiest in the world. In contrast, Singapore boasts one of the highest GDPs per capita in the world and models an exemplary system of education, and yet is home to one of the least positive-minded populations. China also is noteworthy, having experienced the greatest economic boom in recent decades, alongside a surprising overall decline in people's "life-satisfaction."[4]

It appears that statistically, what actually constitutes joy or happiness within a specific people group may be somewhat obscured and not as easily defined as we might think. Regarding the Kingdom of God, it remains crystal clear that righteousness, peace, and joy, are its statistical markers, and there is an all-access and abundant supply.

A *TIME* magazine article makes an interesting observation regarding happiness in culture:

> No American simply inherits happiness by dint of genes or birthplace or a brain set to sunny. Happiness for a culture, is more like a vital sign, the temperature and heart rate of a nation. Like all vital signs, it can fluctuate. But like all vital signs it has a set point, a level to which it strives to return.[5]

LAUGHTER

According to the Harvard Mahoney Neuroscience Institute,[6] studies over the last forty years indicate that laughter has incredible benefits not only emotionally, but also for our physical bodies. Laughter is proven to relieve tension and stress through increasing the activity in antibodies and immune cells, and by improving blood flow and blood vessel function that can help reduce the risk of heart attacks and strokes. There is also scientific proof that triggering the brain's reward and emotional centers through laughter, causes a release of dopamine which aids our brain in processing certain emotional responses and helps regulate pain and stress.

Research at the University of Oxford has also proven that "Laughter with friends releases endorphins, the brain's 'feel-good chemicals,'"[7] which can help raise pain-threshold levels in our physical bodies. Other similar research affirms that laughter plays "a critical role in buffering us against the effects of physiological and psychological stress."[8]

According to the *PsychiatricTimes.com,* "The field of medicine has long recognized the importance of humor. In the 1300s, Henri de Mondeville, a professor of surgery, propagated postoperative therapy with humor"[9]; and in modern times, the Mayo Clinic also affirms that laughter not only lightens our mental load, but also produces measurable physiological changes in our bodies.[10]

According to the Mayo Clinic, laughter has great short-term affects, and data is mounting to show that it not only lightens our load mentally, but also induces physical changes in our bodies.

The short-term benefits of laughter include:

- Stimulation of vital organs. By improving the intake of oxygen-rich air, laughter stimulates lungs, heart, and muscles, and also increases endorphin levels released by the brain.[11]

- Activation and relief of stress response. Deep laughter increases and then decreases heart rate, which enhances and then "cools down" our stress response; resulting in feeling more relaxed.[12]

- Soothing tension. Laughter can also reduce some of the physical symptoms of stress through stimulating circulation and aiding muscle relaxation.[13]

Laughter and joy are part of the more wonderful side of life, and all people have experienced laughter at one time or another that simply overtook us and overwhelmed us. If we think about a good "belly laugh" for more than a moment, we actually want to go back there because we just instinctively *know* that it is a good thing. However, science is telling us that it is actually good *for* us.

Some of the long-term benefits of joy and laughter cited by the Mayo Clinic include how laughter may contribute to:

- Improvement of the immune system. "Negative thoughts manifest into chemical reactions' that can adversely affect our bodies and decreasing our immunity. In contrast, "positive thoughts" can activate neuropeptides in our bodies that that actually help fight stress.[14]

- Relief of pain. Helping the body to produce its own natural "painkillers," laughter may help ease physical pain.[15]

- Mood Improvement. Laughter can elevate mood and help lessen anxiety and depression, often experienced due to difficult situations.[16]

And an article in the *PsychiatricTimes.com* reveals that "laughter is a physical expression of humor and joy that has numerous protective qualities"[17] including:

- Improved Brain Function. Research has proven that humor and happiness contribute to improvement in brain function; "humor releases brain derived neurotrophic factor, which supports existing neurons and encourages the growth of new neurons and synapses."[18]

- Improved Sleep Function. Research has shown that "ten minutes of laughter [can] result in two hours of pain free sleep."[19]

- Affects Vital Body Functions. "Laughter lowers blood pressure, epinephrine, and glucose levels, and increase glucose tolerance."[20]

- Disease Prevention. Laughter is claimed to "assist in the recovery and prevention of cancer by increasing natural killer cell activity."[21]

- Help Revise Past Narratives. "Humor can enhance the willingness to change and improve emotional expectations and can revise habitual narratives that perpetuate shame, hurt, isolation, inferiority, sadness, worry, and perfectionism."[22]

In light of contemporary research, it is incredible that for thousands of years, the God of all wisdom has been urging those who belong to Him to return to joy. Often a command. Always for our good. We were designed to resonate with and live in joy—and scientific research is confirming this truth, shouting loudly to us from the laboratory that we can and should be joyful.

A merry heart does good, like medicine, but a broken spirit dries the bones (Proverbs 17:22).

Researchers from the Royal Society observe that laughter is very different to other nonverbal communication as it is proven to release what they refer to as "euphoric states," in a similar way to dancing, community music-making, and what researchers call "religious practices."[23]

Euphoric means to be marked by a feeling of great happiness or excitement. Some of the synonyms are descriptive and help us see more: ecstatic, enraptured, elated, exhilarated, intoxicated. I think it is safe to say that this sounds a lot like an extended description of joy.

It is amazing that scientific research points to laughter *releasing* and *resulting in* euphoria as well as being a natural outcome of it. Meaning, laughter is not just something that we do when we are already feeling joyful; but scientifically, laughter along with singing, community music-making, and "religious practices,"[24] actually contribute to increasing joy levels in our bodies. God has seemingly inbuilt a cyclical process where we respond to joyful stimulus, engage in laughter, which physiologically produces a natural euphoria, which in turn produces more laughter. A cycle of joy coming from the Father, which ultimately returns to Him in adoration, praise, gratitude, and a lot of joy.

LIFESTYLE

We are becoming increasingly familiar with the necessity to lean into lifestyle choices that support our well-being: watching what we eat, getting adequate sleep, and exercising whether we want to or not. Emotional and mental health have also been widely accepted as aspects of life to measure and be aware of. But are we truly tuned in to everyday patterns that contribute to or detract from joy?

In the *TIME* magazine article, "The Happiness of Pursuit," the question is posed, "How does a brain bred for the joy of pursuit react to stress and a climate of near constant distractions—both grindingly consistent features of the postindustrial world?"[25]

Neuroscientist Sylvia Morelli of Stanford University and psychologist Matt Lieberman of UCLA conducted research to compare empathy levels when people were both purposefully distracted or free to concentrate. The dramatically different results revealed an impairment in the ability to empathize and connect in those who were distracted with memorizing an eight-digit number versus those who were free to focus. The conclusion of the study confirmed that those who responded under an increased "cognitive load" had impaired empathy reactions—but those who were free to engage, whose brains were "uncluttered," felt and processed things more deeply. Morelli states, "Being distracted reduces our empathy for others and blunts responses in the brain. So it's possible that being distracted may also reduce our own happiness."[26]

In our pervasive, multitasking, digital media world, the tendency to live consistently with overloaded brains without regarding the outcome or affect upon our empathetic or joy level is at epidemic proportions. As much as technology is accelerating our productivity, the very drain upon our emotional reserves may actually be taking us farther *away from* the depths of creativity and innovation that the digital age makes more accessible to us.

According to Emma Seppälä, PhD, in her book *The Happiness Track,* "In the race to find what we actually think will ultimately bring us joy, we're actually hurting our chances at getting there."[27] Research has revealed that remaining present in the moment, instead of constantly being distracted by what needs to be done next, actually makes us more productive and happier. A Harvard University study of 5,000 people revealed that "adults spend only about 50% of their time in the present moment"; and research concluded that "when we are in the present moment, we are also at our happiest, no matter what we are doing."[28] This points us toward slowing down, attempting to be present in the moment, and taking a "technology fast," from time to time as Seppälä suggests, to make room for more joy in our lives.

The influence of money and fame also have an effect upon our joy levels. A study led by Edward Deiner at the University of Illinois in 2012 analyzed the responses of 806,526 people in 135 countries collected over the course of six years. It found that "income corresponds more or less directly to happiness but only if a person's wealth and aspirations keep pace."[29] In the current climate of social media and reality shows, we all get to see into the private lives of the famous and wealthy, and so we all "suffer by comparison" to someone.

Another interesting quote from the *TIME* article titled, "The Happiness of Pursuit" by Jeffrey Kluger clarifies this point further:

> In the *TIME* poll, 60% of respondents said they do not feel better about themselves after spending time on social media, and 76% believe other people make themselves look happier, more attractive and more successful than they actually are on their Facebook page.[30]

An in-depth study at the University of California Berkeley compared the difference between socioeconomic status (a mathematical measure of income), and sociometric status (a comparison with the people around you). The results of the study showed that in the era of social media, the tension between the two has "accelerated dramatically" due to comparison and dissatisfaction.[31] Scripture is clear that the *love of money* is the problem, not money itself.[32] The problem for us here is not necessarily the accumulation of wealth, but the unfortunate wedding of our possessions with our identity.

According to research, close relationships and the important issue of how we relate to others are also shown to be influential on our capacity for joy. Statistics reveal that the happiest people have lots of healthy social relationships as a common element, relying on what psychologists call "social snacking," or multiple ways of connecting with fellow human beings.[33] Other studies have revealed that when a person focuses on endeavoring to make a significant person in their life happier, the result is that the giver also becomes significantly happier.[34] Close meaningful relationships shape our joy framework and contribute to our own sense of satisfaction and joy.

Bryan Walsh's article, "Does Spirituality Makes Us Happy?" reveals interesting statistics regarding the Church in the United States:

> "Without that sense of community, religion may not be as strong a protector against unhappiness. In a survey of U.S. adults conducted in 2006 and 2007, researchers led by sociologist Chaeyoon Lim of the University of Wisconsin–Madison found that 33% of those who attended religious services every week and reported having close friends at church said they were extremely satisfied with their lives, while only 19% of those who went to church but had no close connections to the congregation reported the same satisfaction."[35]

The subject of gratitude and thanks is a massive theme in the Bible that is repeated over and over again; and scientific research affirms that gratitude contributes significantly to levels of joy and happiness. Secular studies show that when we are regularly grateful and acknowledge "goodness in life," we are generally happier and healthier than our counterparts. Psychologists also affirm that expressing gratitude for "people and experiences, rather than things" produces the most bliss.[36]

These findings are astounding to me, revealing what God has said in multiple ways throughout the ages. The fascinating study of Brain Science has further insights into joy for us.

BRAIN SCIENCE

One of the primary discoveries in the arena of brain science is the importance of returning to joy, which takes us back to the root word *rejoice* and how developed we are in our capacity to quickly return to joy in adverse circumstances.[37]

You may be familiar with the basic concepts of left brain and right brain differences, namely that the left side of our brain is mainly involved with problem solving; and the right side involves relationships and nonverbal processing. Contrary to popular opinion, the right side of our brain actually processes faster and responds first; whereas the left side of our brain is actually slower and secondary. Those who are primarily right-sided "creatives" are finally vindicated!

The right side of the brain learns primarily from mirroring rather than truth statements, and is more intuitive. It is *subconsciously trained and shaped through interaction rather than information*. In contrast, the left side of the brain focuses upon truth and choices, responding to verbal communication, but is interestingly *non-relational*, processing in a way that *does not create attachments to people*. This research has uncovered that we cannot think our way to an attachment with people or with God. Let's pause and reflect on that for a moment.

Another fascinating truth is that our brains run on one of two primary fuel options—*fear or joy*. It is interesting that our brains are designed to grow healthily, and function primarily fueled by joy. In contrast, fear creates one of three primal instincts—fight, flight, or freeze—none of which are conducive to the fullness of life that Jesus wants for us.

Remarkably, the science behind our brains tells us that the attachment part of our brain looks for joy *everywhere*—searches it out—and when we cannot find it, we will be prompted to return to predictable experiences, places, or substances to provide it. When someone comes along and awakens joy in us that we are not receiving elsewhere, we will be attracted and vulnerable to it. This carries so many ramifications for the healing of unhealthy addictions, the temptation for affairs outside of marriage, and reinforces the inescapable reality that we are created for connection with God and His joy, and relationship with others.

Another interesting finding is that the "action center" of our brain contains what can be likened to a joy container that can actually *grow in capacity over time*. Research has revealed that the extent of our emotional capacity equals our capacity for joy; and furthermore, the greater our capacity for joy, the greater the capacity not to be overwhelmed.

Studies have shown that *developing and practicing* habits of appreciation enhances the bandwidth of our joy. Developing a *habit to enjoy things*—that is, moving beyond commenting on a beautiful sunset to *actually stopping for a moment to appreciate it*—releases powerful brain-altering results. Giving ourselves *permission to experience* moments of joy causes our capacity for joy to increase. Our brains learn that if joy is possible, it can return there anytime. Experiencing joy and sharing it with others then, causes joy multiplication that is not only emotional but literally brain changing.

The following five simple suggestions for increasing our capacity for joy are:

- Asking yourself, what is going on in the present that I can appreciate?
- Asking yourself, what am I looking forward to?
- Intentionally cataloging joy-filled memories and revisiting them regularly.
- Experiencing joy in community.
- Playing some of your favorite songs.

Brain science reaffirms what the Father has encouraged us to do all along. Returning to joy is a God concept that we can train our brains to do every day. Will you join me?

> *Further, my brothers and sisters, rejoice in the Lord! It is no trouble for me to write the same things to you again, and it is a safeguard for you. Watch out for those dogs, those evildoers, those mutilators of the flesh. For it is we who are the circumcision, we who serve God by his Spirit, who boast in Christ Jesus, and who put no confidence in the flesh* (Philippians 3:1-3 NIV).

The science of joy is fascinating. From the physiological effects and health benefits of laughter and humor upon our bodies and emotions, the repercussions of mental clutter and living in the moment, to the importance of relationships and gratitude. It all makes so much sense. The wiring of our brains means that we default to searching for fear or joy and look for attachments and relationships that spark joy for us. Scientific research reminds us that we were made to live consistently connected to the joy of God, and the God of joy.

• • •

REDISCOVERING JOY: STEP 7

Engage in Prayer

> *Father, You are the incredible Master Craftsman, the Creator, and Originator of all intelligent design in the universe. Thank You that scientific research is proving who You are, the truth You have revealed in Your Word to us, and how we function as people You have created. Father, it's my desire to laugh more than I have before. I want to lean into lifestyle choices that maximize well-being and limit all unhealthy distractions, letting go of whatever circumvents Your plan for full joy both in and through me. Teach me to cultivate, treasure, and feed healthy patterns of relationship and community modeled by You, in order to walk in greater wholeness, and the picture of abundant life that You have in Your heart for me.*

Reflection

- Reflect upon how quickly you are able to return to joy after taking a hit or navigating a challenging situation. Are there specific circumstances or types of challenge that are particularly resistant to you rebounding to a place of joy? Consider what tools the Father wants to give to you to break this cycle and spring back more consistently.

- How much room do you make for laughter in your life? Take time to reflect upon your work-life balance and how much space you dedicate to life-giving celebration and recreation. Are the activities you dedicate your spare time to actually refreshing or depleting you? List some fun activities to do with friends or family that might be outside of your comfort zone.

Activation

- Proactively engage in a negativity fast, covering thoughts, words, attitudes, and actions. Be ruthless in catching and reversing out of engagement with negativity. Partner with Holy Spirit in what He wants to do to replace and reinvent the places that may have been overgrown with negativity. Replace the old patterns of responding negatively with truth from God's heart, and a new perspective built on how He sees things.

- Consider a technology fast or reduce your smartphone use. Repurpose your time to engage in activities that refresh you, build key relationships, or intentionally build toward the preferable future God is revealing to you. Decide to be more present in the moment when around family and friends, listening more intentionally and responding more fully.

- Engage with the five listed Brain Science steps to develop and practice habits of appreciation. Give yourself permission to experience joy. This will produce changes in your brain patterns that physiologically increase your capacity for joy!

8

Atmosphere

*A*ccording to Merriam-Webster, the definition of *atmosphere* is: a surrounding or pervading mood, environment, or influence; the dominant mood or emotional tone, a distinctive quality. Some of its synonyms are: tone, mood, feel, sense, ambience, climate.

Stewarding our own personal atmosphere[1] is one of the greatest callings we have as followers of Jesus, becoming increasingly like Him and reflecting His presence from the inside out. However, simply maintaining personal joy, although crucial, is not to mark the *limit or boundary* of the manifestation of joy that God intends for our world. It is true that He is absolutely committed to furnishing each of us with abundant and unending joy—remember that Jesus said our joy would be full and would remain—but this is not a place for us to stop and set up camp. We are designed to move beyond simply preserving joy for our own lives and *rise to become joy catalysts who change things in our sphere of authority*. We have full permission to be both receivers and dispensers of His joy.

As we have explored, there is a progression to the outfolding of joy that comes from the Father and into our world. Our God of joy, creating *from* joy and relating to us *in* joy, has invited us into coworking with Him in stewarding a Kingdom of righteousness, peace, and joy that is resident within us *but then overflows* to transform the world around us in glorious ways. This makes joy so much more than an unpredictable emotion. The joy we have access to is a powerful force of *personal* renewal and restoration, but also a catalytic force of *societal* renewal and reformation.

The discussion then, should center on how to make room for environments both personally and organizationally that *cultivate, activate, and multiply* atmospheres of God's intended joy. There are many ways to illustrate how this can happen, and many models have been successful in seeing healthy environments emerge that operate as "greenhouses" for what the Father wants to produce. The following progression is one way to think about the process of moving into a joy-filled culture and pervading atmosphere:

The joy inherent in God being Himself,

Creates an inward reality of joy in individuals,

Who develop core values and practices that reflect
and model His joy,

That shape environments or cultures that
multiply joy,

Producing a pervading atmosphere of joy that
influences beyond itself.

Or more simply put, the joy of God creates an inward reality, generating core values and practices that shape a culture of joy, producing a pervading atmosphere.

These phases will represent different things for an individual versus a church or organization. For some, it may be simple to identify which stage you are in and where to focus next. Alternatively, for others, some deeper reflection will be needed to bring insight as to where you are on the joy timeline. The current season may be requiring you to reclaim joy in your personal life; or you may have joy established on the inside and are cultivating core values around that. You may be a leader who is positioned to shape the environment or culture of your organization. Whatever your role or season, God wants to release a deluge of joy that carries transformational possibility for you and everything you come in contact with!

HEAVEN'S ATMOSPHERE

We have talked extensively about the joy that exists because of God just being God, with everything starting with Him. Before exploring environments that multiply joy, I want to bring into focus our interaction with the spiritual realm and remind ourselves what the atmosphere surrounding God Himself looks like. In using the word *atmosphere,* the dictionary definition helps us to think in terms of a surrounding or pervading influence, tone, ambience, or climate. Abstract terms that are not necessarily easy to tie down, but nevertheless ones that should be very real to us as those who are created as spirit beings who also happen live in physical bodies.

Scripture is full of accounts of people who had encounters with God and His realm, and under the inspiration of the Holy Spirit described these moments that have become part of God's Word to us for generations. The opening verse of the book of Ezekiel says clearly, "…the heavens were opened and I saw visions of God" (Ezekiel 1:1 NIV). He proceeds to describe an incredible encounter that includes a fire-filled windstorm, four living creatures with four faces and four wings, a wheel within a wheel, and a vision of God as glowing metal, fire, and surrounded by brilliant light.[2]

One of Ezekiel's most well-known visions describes God's presence as a river that influences everything it touches (see Ezekiel 47), and we will explore this more later in the chapter. Similarly, the first six chapters of the book of Zechariah are comprised almost entirely of a series of visions, dreams, and encounters. His experiences include: symbolic visions of four horns that symbolize empires (Zechariah 1:18); visions of two golden pipes that pour out golden oil and a flying scroll (Zechariah 4:12; 5:1); and four chariots that represent the four spirits of Heaven (Zechariah 6:1-8); as well as ongoing question and answer sessions with angelic beings (Zechariah 1:9; 2:3; 4:2,11; 5:2).

There are other examples in Scripture such as Daniel's dreams and visions and the numerous dreams, angelic visitations, and encounters that surrounded the birth of Jesus,[3] and the powerful interaction between Heaven and earth that impacted the early Church.[4] All of this speaks to the reality that we live in a supernatural relationship with the realm of God. The truth is, God lives in and moves *from* the unseen, *into* the seen.[5] It is a principle of the Kingdom.

> *So we look not at the things which are seen, but at the things which are unseen; for the things which are visible are temporal [just brief and fleeting], but the things which are invisible are everlasting and imperishable* (2 Corinthians 4:18 AMP).
>
> *By faith we understand that the universe was created by the word of God, so that what is seen was not made out of things that are visible* (Hebrews 11:3 ESV).

As followers of Jesus, we simultaneously interact with what is both visible and invisible. Scripture clearly informs us that what is unseen is actually more real than that which *we* call reality. We are simultaneously both seated with Him in heavenly realms (Ephesians 2:3-6) and seated here on earthly chairs. In praying, "Your kingdom come and will be done on earth as it is in Heaven," we are echoing generations that have gone before: "Come, Father, as You are, and invade earth with Your ways, heart, and very presence; come with Your atmosphere so that our atmosphere looks more like Yours."

There are many other descriptions about the atmosphere of Heaven revealed in Scripture. In examples from the book of Revelation,[6] the images are provoking. There is no need for light because His presence is like the brightest sun, thousands of angels respond in adoration to the revealing of His presence twenty-four hours a day, the knowledge of the overcoming and finished work of Jesus is celebrated, there is Heaven to earth interaction, singing, shouts and noise is prevalent, there are no more tears or sorrow, a victorious ending to the story of history, and all things are made new. What kind of atmospheric reality does all of this stir up for you? I want to shout, "YES!"

Even with the reality of Heaven's atmosphere being so clear for us both in Scripture and experience, we can sometimes miss or misinterpret moments from God.

> *"Now My soul is troubled, and what shall I say? 'Father, save Me from this hour'? But for this purpose I came to this hour. Father, glorify Your name." Then a voice came from heaven, saying, "I have both glorified it and will glorify it again." Therefore, the people who stood by and heard it said that it had thundered. Others said, "An angel has spoken to Him"* (John 12:27-29).

When Jesus hears the voice of the Father here, there is an interesting response from those around Him who *also heard*. God can be speaking and working in a powerful way, but people may not perceive it, or even totally miss that it is God who is moving. When God spoke, some who were near thought that it had thundered, a natural phenomenon, and others thought that it was angelic, a spiritualized phenomenon. Neither were correct. Some of the most beautiful things that God will do and say through His presence with us will be interpreted as natural or vaguely supernatural, but not attributed to or accepted as Him, even among some who are near.

Like many others, I have personally experienced encounters with God and His realm that have altered the course of my life. Dreams, visions, angelic encounters, visitations, divine protection; most I don't ever talk about, although some contain information that I have acted upon or communicated to those it relates to. Usually these moments are not something I am actively seeking, but often require a *leaning into the invitation* and a *posture of receiving* in order to step into the moment.

I want you to perceive and see with me; allow the Holy Spirit to reveal to you what is beyond words or explanation. Access and interaction with the spiritual realm is part of our inheritance and normal for us when we are born again.[7] Paul prays that the eyes of our hearts would be enlightened, and that we would carry a spirit of wisdom and revelation in the knowledge of God.[8] Jesus "saw" what His Father was doing;[9] John on the Island of Patmos saw a "door open in Heaven" and heard a voice that said, "Come up here."[10] God is asking us to see something that is *not* natural. He is asking us to make room for Him and His atmosphere that is more real than anything we see or perceive here in the earthly dimension.

Many people joke that we can become so heavenly minded that we are of no earthy good, but could it be that the opposite is also true? That we can at times be so earthly minded, that our heavenly interaction is diminished? We have numerous, wonderful, practical seminars, workshops, and events that champion how to function more effectively and efficiently as individuals and organizations. These are impactful and necessary to help build infrastructure around the life that God is releasing, but are *only components, not the whole picture,* as we move forward. Let us again begin to see and perceive Heaven's atmosphere in a dynamic, life-altering way and hunger for it as a necessity.

We must experience the Father and His atmosphere before we can ever give it away. Remember that the Holy Spirit is available as our interface and connection with the Father. That is why He was sent, and why He lives in everyone who belongs to Jesus. Remember, experiencing the joy of God and the atmosphere of Heaven is not something that we access through our left-brain logic. Giving yourself permission to experience God and leaning into Him is all that is needed. He can do a lot with simple availability. Take a moment to pray and respond. No matter how long you have known Him, there is always more to experience and see. God's facets are limitless.

> *...For the Spirit searches everything, even the depths of God. For who knows a person's thoughts except the spirit of that person, which is in him? So also no one comprehends the thoughts of God except the Spirit of God. Now we have received not the spirit of the world, but the Spirit who is from God, that we might understand the things freely given us by God* (1 Corinthians 2:10-12 ESV).

PERSONAL ATMOSPHERE

We explored the working of the inward presence of God in the "Inside Out" chapter, acknowledging the Holy Spirit as our interface with God's presence. We are all gifted differently and have unique callings and spheres of influence according to the Father's design; but ultimately, these are all developed from the *inside out*. Remember that the fruit of the Spirit ministers to *us* first, and *then* becomes an inward reality so that we are those who intuitively walk in love, joy, peace, patience, kindness, goodness, faithfulness, and self-control.

Along with the Word of God, discipleship, community, prayer, and personal time with God, the indwelling presence of Holy Spirit becomes the foundation for the atmosphere inside us. We allow the ways of God and the nature and character of the Spirit of God to overshadow us and transform us; and the Kingdom of righteousness, peace, and joy that is within us becomes established.

As we continue to grow, we learn to steward the inward reality of God's presence and this becomes the place of authority from which we move into everything that He wants to invite us into. We don't really ever move away from cultivating and stewarding the inward life of God. Remember that Jesus said without *remaining* in Him, we could do nothing.[11]

Because we are focused on personal atmosphere in this section, I want to share with you something of my own internal reality in walking with Jesus. Having always been *hardwired* to discern and feel atmospheres—something that I did not chose or work hard to develop—it has been an interesting journey in understanding this part of my call and gifting that was simply just present from a very early age. Crafted by God, formed and known to Him before I was born,[12] I later came to understand that two operational gifts on my life were the prophetic, particularly in the seer dimension and the discerning of spirits,[13] which as we explored, describes a perception and concern with the complete bandwidth of the spiritual dimension. Interaction with the spiritual realm is quite real and natural for me, and can manifest in multiple ways:

- Seeing (pictures, dreams, visions, encounters)

- Knowing (past, present, and future information, the counsel of God, wisdom)
- Sensing (atmospheres in geographic areas, dominant spiritual forces, joy, sorrow, the state of the soul)
- Hearing (God's voice, angelic communication and singing, Holy Spirit, other people's thoughts)
- Feeling (dimensions of God's presence, anointings, atmospheres, angelic and demonic realms)

These simply highlight some ways in which I relate to God personally from the inside out, which affects my personal core values and practices and therefore shapes the culture of my life and leadership focus. Others burn on the inside with discovering theological truth in Scripture, delving into the original languages of Hebrew and Greek, and others have a pastoring gift that literally moves them from the inside out. There is room for all of God and the many ways that He loves to work.

Although born with a propensity toward the gift-mix that I have described, the Holy Spirit, pastors, and mentors have enabled the expansion and understanding of my personal gifting over time. Some encounters with the heavenly realm have caused my gift to accelerate, others heightened my spiritual perceptions, and others increased my sensitivity to the Holy Spirit in certain areas. Other encounters with God actually inaugurated or activated certain giftings and workings inside me that have never left. Learning to lean into encounters with God has been an imperative component in expanding from the inside out and receiving the fullness of all that He has in His heart for me.

• • •

The global renewal[14] movement is multifaceted with many tributaries and is not easily defined or neatly contained in a specific box. Growing out of the seedbed of the charismatic movement, it has certain distinctives and identifiable traits. It is a movement that has wonderfully normalized life in the Spirit and provided places for the Body of Christ to expand their *inward life* and capacity in God. Extended praise and worship, lingering in God's presence, soaking or resting in the Spirit, soaking prayer, fire-tunnels, impartation, laughing in the Spirit, to name just some, are practices that have made room for personal interaction with the atmosphere of God's presence. This has resulted in many identifiable outcomes for the Body of Christ:

- Personal and powerful encounters with God.
- Experiencing increased dimensions of God's love, peace, and favor.
- A relational rather than intellectual paradigm in walking with God.
- An increased capacity for more of God's presence.
- Learning how to position ourselves to receive from God.
- Interaction and familiarity with the movings of Holy Spirit.
- Increased sensitivity to God's presence and His voice.
- Activation of spiritual gifts.
- Activation of supernatural joy.

Powerful interactions with God have normalized the Presence-led life. Many encounters can be categorized under the "soaking – moving – explosive" categories outlined earlier; but the list and the outcomes are just a starting place to highlight what God has been doing through renewal. Millions in the Body of Christ have been impacted to expand on the inside, experiencing and encountering God in new and illuminating ways. Many have never been the same.

The activation of supernatural joy is a key encounter for us to experience, for all of the reasons we have explored in the book so far. It also begins with an internal impartation from Holy Spirit, who carries the joy of the Kingdom. Let's look further at a key Scripture that helps shed some light on expanding in joy on the inside:

> *And don't get drunk with wine, which is rebellion; instead be filled with the fullness of the Holy Spirit* (Ephesians 5:18 TPT).

There are several intriguing aspects to this passage. First, Paul compares getting drunk with wine to being filled with the Spirit. Being very clear about excess alcohol, but instructing us *instead,* to be filled with the Holy Spirit. In order to get physically drunk, someone would have to purposefully and deliberately lean into drinking more than they should. There is an intentionality that accompanies this, and there are certain outcomes in behavior; these can be negative including violence, neglect, economic failure in the long term, among others. There are also alcohol-induced feelings and emotions that accompany drunkenness. These are *artificially created* states as a result of alcohol;

but Paul compares the two, and points us back to the release of true joy, freedom, and liberty through deliberately drinking of the Holy Spirit.

This is not an easy discussion for many, especially as the results of alcohol abuse are very real to many and those they love; but nevertheless, important to open out in a book dedicated to the subject of joy. I want to be clear that I am *not* advocating physical drunkenness because it will *not* give us *true* joy, freedom, or a sense of liberty. I am using it as an example of a counterfeit, to compare what God really wants to give us by His Spirit. This is in fact what the apostle Paul was saying.

"Holy laughter" has been a manifestation of the Holy Spirit seen in many of the great historic revivals, and has its biblical premise in such passages as Ephesians 5:18, and also the day of Pentecost when those who are gathered around the phenomenon of the outpouring of the Holy Spirit accuse the followers of Jesus of being drunk (Acts 2:13).

Peter addresses the crowd and assures them that what they are seeing is not a result of wine but is a fulfillment of what was spoken by the prophet Joel (see Joel 2:15-16). We cannot prove exactly what unfolded as God poured out Himself, but something was happening beyond speaking in new languages, that caused those in the crowd to believe that "new wine" was the culprit. The most important thing is that the resurrected presence of Jesus was there, and 3,000 were added to the Body of Christ; the Church was birthed and would change the world.

It is crucial to open out the issue of drinking of the Holy Spirit, because there are dimensions of God's joy that we have not tasted or experienced, facets of joy that exist in Him that will literally transform the darkest and most depleted places it encounters. We may have settled for a measure of joy, or comfortable, usual expressions of joy that we have encountered before. When Paul invites us to be *filled with the fullness* of the Holy Spirit, this is speaking in terms of being saturated with the third person of the Godhead. By default, this changes our internal atmosphere, the internal environment of our lives, which in turn changes how we walk, talk, respond, laugh, and live as those who are His.

Maybe you have been closed to new encounters with the Holy Spirit, offended by things you have seen in renewal gatherings, or skeptical about the Presence-filled life. I personally decided a long time ago that I wanted everything God intended to give me, whether I understood it or not, and I would trust Him to reveal truth through His Word regarding the reality of His ways, encounters, and atmosphere. I am convinced that His ability to hold on to me is greater than my ability to hold on to Him; and His Word literally says that as a good Father, He will give us the Spirit liberally, if we ask.[15]

The reality of being forgiven, restored to relationship with God, and spending eternity with Him should fill us with joy daily. But because God is the everlasting, uncaused, self-existent One, the self-sufficient, self-sustaining, luminous, radiant One, the supply of Heaven will *never* be depleted, and the invitation for us to encounter more of Him will *always* be there. Please take a moment to stop and digest what has been shared. Welcome the presence of the Holy Spirit to meet with you, and whether you are a renewal veteran or new to the Presence-infused life, allow Him to release a fresh wind over you, drink deeply of Him, and let Him invite you into more than you have ever encountered before.

SUPERNATURAL ATMOSPHERE

Having established a place for the consistent pursuit of personal renewal, we want to consider what it looks like for God's presence to then *flow through us* in a supernatural way—changing things around us to look more like Heaven. The Kingdom is within us in order to get out of us, and an atmosphere change is simply an outward expression of an inward reality. God is the Giver and we live as those who are dispensers of all that He is giving. Joy is not primarily *for* you but given to *flow through you*. He rests on you for the benefit of the world.

> *On the last and greatest day of the festival, Jesus stood and said in a loud voice, "Let anyone who is thirsty come to me and drink. Whoever believes in me, as Scripture has said, rivers of living water will flow from within them." By this he meant the Spirit, whom those who believed in him were later to receive...* (John 7:37-40 NIV).

Jesus uses a river analogy to describe the flow of the Holy Spirit through our lives. When water overflows its container and into the infrastructure around it, we call it leaking. The Spirit of God within you is designed to move outward and touch those around you. *You are created to leak.* We know that the apostles laid their hands on the sick and they recovered,[16] just as Jesus promised that they would.[17] This describes an impartation of the Holy Spirit from the inside out. Scripture also tells us that the sick were placed on the street so that Peter's shadow could heal them,[18] and that unusual miracles were done through cloth that touched Paul:

*And God was doing extraordinary miracles by the hands
of Paul, so that even handkerchiefs or aprons that had
touched his skin were carried away to the sick, and their
diseases left them and the evil spirits came out of them*
(Acts 19:11 ESV).

These are supernatural instances of the transfer of God's presence. Similarly, the woman with the issue of blood who *touched* Jesus clothes,[19] caused Him to realize that *power went out from him*, even though surrounded by crowds of people. He was curious to know who had touched Him and made a *withdrawal* on the power of the Spirit that was resident within Him.[20] Impartation can occur as a result of our *intentional releasing it for purpose*, or when someone *pulls from* the presence of God that is upon our lives. Just like dimensions of healing, supernatural peace, and love, joy can be experienced not only *by us* but *through us and around us.*

I've personally received impartation of supernatural, unexplainable joy from the Holy Spirit, often directly, but also through receiving prayer in various ways. At times, I have been overtaken by and overwhelmed by joy in a way that was impossible to manufacture, and sometimes for hours at a time. There have been moments in my life when it was possible to measure a distinct emotional difference before and after such experiences. Joy remained. A residue, an afterglow, a permanent presence.

Not surprisingly, imparting the Father's joy to others in prayer has become a resident gift upon my life, so that now praying for joy is normal, and seeing people touched by God's joy is expected. May an unusual expectation and faith for giving away the joy of the Kingdom that lives in you rise in your life and mark the beginning of a dreaming with God of all the ways that His surprising joy is waiting to impact those around you.

I am beyond convinced of the atmosphere of life and joy that we are designed to carry as children of God. It is an impossibility for the One who defeated death and hell, who gave us a regenerated nature, and actually lives in us and through us by His Spirit to not change the atmosphere around us when we enter an environment. It's inconceivable that the same Spirit who raised Christ from the dead cannot dispel darkness in whatever way it is manifesting in a particular situation.

Scripture is filled with numerous stories of individuals and groups becoming overtaken by the atmosphere of the presence of God. One specific example is the spirit of prophecy that overtakes Saul when he meets the company of prophets coming down from the high places, so that he prophesies until morning, becoming changed into a different person.[21]

This gives us insight that the pervading gift upon the group (in this instance, prophecy) became the expression of the pervading atmosphere that surrounded them, so that other individuals could then experience it. The spirit of prophecy resting upon the company of prophets became the primary atmosphere that Saul encountered; and just like the spirit of prophecy in this account, a spirit of joy can show up in a room or geographic location, changing the atmosphere and inviting us to be changed into a different person. The fact that this is an Old Testament account, before the Spirit of God was resident in every born-again believer, makes it more astonishing and powerful to me. How much more now, can the atmosphere of God—filled with love, peace, hope, authority, righteousness, and joy—emanate from us and touch the world around us?

One well known but incredible image serves as fuel for revelation regarding the release of the Spirit of God in our lives, communities, and cities. Ezekiel's vision of the river of God in chapter 47 has been a powerful symbolic image capturing my own imagination, and the hearts of Jesus followers for centuries. Ezekiel is introduced to the river of God in a vision, which is depicted as flowing out of the Old Testament temple and gets measurably deeper as he is led out into the water, eventually becoming deep enough to swim in. The outcome is a life that is underwater.

This speaks to me of a saturation in the things of God, submerged in the presence of God—a life carried along by and defined by the river of God's Spirit. Ezekiel goes on to speak of saltwater becoming fresh, with swarms of living creatures that flourish everywhere the river flows. A staggering statement is central to Ezekiel's encounter, "everything will live wherever the river flows."[22] Everything. Will. Live. What a statement and a promise. Not only depleted places are destined to become fresh, but *dead things that are seemingly without hope live* because of the presence of God.

What does a life look like that is saturated by the Spirit and the atmosphere of God? Thoughts, emotions, motives, words, actions, responses? The symbolism of this life-giving river moves from imagination to reality, from internal probability to external possibility when Jesus announced that there would be a resident river flowing *from* those who are His. Everything can live. Everything will live. The one who demonstrated life itself, transforming sick and diseased bodies, and raising the dead, ventures into the revealing of the Father's delight—that not only would we belong to Him, but we would co-work with Him to see His life bring fantastic transformation. As if wanting to live in us was not amazing enough, He goes further to say that He wants live *through* us just as Jesus experienced. We become not just recipients of life, but distributors. Brokers of heavenly realities.

Ezekiel's vision also expands further. It reveals that fruit trees of all kinds grow on both banks of this incredible river, and their leaves do not wither, their fruit does not fail. Every month they bear fruit, and this fruit serves as food, and the leaves for healing. The flow of the river of God *produces a permanent fruitfulness that is not dependent on earthly seasons*, a sustained and unfailing fruitfulness that releases life to everything it touches. The very presence of the Spirit of God with us is designed to produce in us a permanent fruitfulness that is undeterred by what season we are in and undiminished by circumstances that would normally result in a withering or failing. It is then given away as sustenance and healing to those who need it. This is what Jesus modeled for us. This is what the early Church modeled for us. This is what we model for the world around us.

The Holy Spirit is still attracted to chaotic, void, dead places, just as in the beginning of creation in the opening verses of the book of Genesis. Everywhere the river goes in your family, workplace, business, school, college, city—there is a promise that everything will live. Bodies will live. Marriages will live. Destiny will live. Potential will live. Mental capacity will thrive. Entrepreneurial foresight and insight will flourish. Vision will emerge. Emotional health will be evident. We are invited into a renewing of our minds regarding what it means for everything to live. This is our mandate.

It does not mean that we will be received by everyone. In fact, Scripture is clear that to some we are the fragrance of life, and to others the fragrance of death[23] as we offer a life that is no longer self-focused or self-feeding. Our God who loves to layer His super over our natural is redefining what is normally possible, what is logically reasonable, and what is usually expected. I don't think that a movement started by the Son who healed lepers, opened blind eyes, and was Himself raised from the dead is aiming at maintaining the status quo, or desiring to quietly fit in. The very nature of God being Himself is disruption to our normal, and an earthquake to our sensibilities. Is He the God of order? Absolutely. Is He the God who can disrupt that order in a nanosecond? Absolutely. He is God, and everywhere His river goes, everything will live.

Jesus was very clear that our enemy comes to steal, kill, and destroy, but that He came to give us life, and life in abundance.[24] It does not take a lot of effort to look at various situations and circumstances and perceive in which column we should place them. Life or death. The Father placed us in an affluent area of our city when we moved to the United States several years ago. There are people, housing estates, and businesses that look incredibly well put together, but just below the surface life is desperately needed. Traveling all around the world, we realize that people everywhere are the same. You have heard it a thousand times, but every individual *does* long to be restored to the fullness of the relationship with their Creator; and everyone whether they know it or not, longs to live and breathe in their Father's presence. We look for anything and everything to fill the void of intimacy with the greatest Father. We all carry a sense of a desire for the restored life, the restored heart, and the restored destiny.

Many who do not yet know Jesus would not name it in this way. But many would agree that things are not the way they should be. We long for life. We were made for life in abundance. As the people of God, you and I carry this desired life in us and get to represent the Father wherever we are positioned by Him, and the promise is that everything will live. It is the very Spirit of God who changes the atmosphere around us so that the desire of nations is with us. But all of this is not just *for us*—He will move mountains with us or without us to reach every person He created with His great love.

What would it be like for us to live intentionally, watching for the whisper of the Father to see what He wants to bring to life in every moment. Someone's dignity. Their hope. Their physical body. Someone's honor. A knowledge of their created design. Their joy. When the Father touches places that have been dead, diminished, and hopeless, and breath comes back into areas of people's lives that were suffocated and without light, the miraculous happens. The response and the result is pure joy. An instinctive, unstoppable, intuitive surge of joy.

The atmosphere that we will allow God to establish in our lives exists for others as well as for ourselves and our families. We get to steward the gifts and callings upon our lives, and what we can refer to as our time, talent, and treasure—but we are also invited to steward the inward atmosphere that rests upon our lives and give it away as a river that brings life. This happens in the simplest ways through proximity in public. Experimenting with this is amazing.

As mentioned earlier, I have the privilege of regularly traveling internationally, and although there are many high points to interfacing with the Body of Christ in person, in different regions, there are also some challenging dynamics to traveling. On a recent flight, an extremely upset baby was not seated far from me. Before I could further entertain the "selfless" thoughts that began involuntarily entering my head such as, "What a wonderful flight this is going to be without sleep," the Holy Spirit asked me a question. It was really more of an invitation. "What if you released My peace?"

I waited a few moments as the crying and volume increased in ferocity. Remembering the anxiety my own wife would often feel on a flight when our own young sons were inconsolable, my heart went out to the amazing mom as well as for my own sanity. I took a breath and whispered, "Peace." Within a few seconds the child settled down and silence filled the cabin. I wasn't shocked, but I did smile at the kindness of God and the answers He loves to bring from the supply of His presence that lives within us.

The baby woke up a number of times; and on each occasion, I continued to release God's peace, and he continued to settle immediately, time after time. Listening for God's invitations is now a hobby of mine. There is joy in partnering with what He wants to do in big and small ways. He may even want to release joy into the lives of some unsuspecting people. Let's pause and think about that.

Imparting joy to the Body of Christ is crucial. Consider your local church for a moment. It is full of trailblazers—teachers, entrepreneurs, parents, doctors, managers, lawyers, architects, administrators, etc.—who are dispensing the Kingdom of God every day with a desire to see Jesus transform their sphere of influence. Seeing them return to joy, and all that it releases in them, is a powerful necessity. The intended joy that Father has for them to walk in is not an insignificant side note, but a supernatural phenomenon. Joy encounters that release joyful sons and daughters *may do more to influence our world in the coming days than anything else.* Joy is vibrant, refreshing, strengthening, contagious, and life giving. Bringing an atmospheric change.

When the Father creates a desire in us to experience certain aspects of His presence not only in our lives, but *through* our lives, we can receive it as a God-given gift from Him—a desire that He wants to fulfill. When He gives us the desires of His heart,[25] they are fulfillments of what He already placed there in seed form. There are numerous stories of those who hungered after healing the sick and prayed for thousands before seeing a breakthrough. They were propelled by an inward desire planted by God that pulled them into accessing manifestations of healing. And breakthrough came.

Likewise, when the Father grants us access to places in Him, or realms of His Kingdom, it is my conviction that He is offering us not only a partnership in the moment, but an invitation to steward that aspect of His governing presence with us, permanently. Consider the manifestations of God's presence that have shown up in or through your life as the Father's acknowledgment of His trust in you, and an invitation to access those places when and where they are needed.

Stop for a moment and ask yourself what the *dominant atmosphere is surrounding your life*, and what aspect of God's presence dominates the atmosphere around you. Take a moment to remember aspects of His presence that have powerfully impacted your life or worked through you to impact others. These are places for you to revisit, dust off, and reengage. If joy is not on the list, consider allowing the Holy Spirit to stir a hunger in you for new experiences with the joy of God that framed the universe, and an atmosphere inside you that can bring joy wherever you find yourself.

CORE VALUES FOR CREATING CULTURES OF JOYFUL TRANSFORMATION

Earlier in the book, we gathered around the understanding that the Body of Christ is moving into a renew, rebuild, restore mandate, emerging out of the context of joyful encounters.[26] This positions us to stand in the personal stewardship of the atmosphere of God on the inside, but ultimately moves us *beyond personal renewal and into the desire for transformation of every sphere of culture*. Beyond the individual, and to the many.

Because it takes a culture to influence a culture, God is inviting us into the formation of environments or cultures that carry His very values, priorities, and presence in transformative dimensions. The culture of death, depression, heaviness, loss, and bitterness is to be influenced by and resurrected through a culture of joy, light, hope, buoyancy, delight, and laughter. Let's revisit again our statement regarding the steps to growing a culture of joy that is capable of catalyzing atmospheric shifts: The joy of God creates an inward reality, generating core values and practices that shape a culture of joy, producing a pervading atmosphere.

The question remains as to how we shape a culture that carries joyful realities with authority to transform everything around it. Pastor and prayer leader Pete Grieg, founder of the global 24-7 Prayer[27] movement, shares several keys that shape a culture. Simply stated, these are:

- The prayers that we pray.
- The stories that we tell.
- The heroes that we hail.
- The people we surround ourselves with.
- The failures that we celebrate.
- The songs that we sing.

What resonates with me here is that each of these ingredients function as *declarers of truth and shapers of belief*—gathering the community around what is to be honored and hallowed, preserved and prized. They are not action steps, goals, or tactical details, but overarching meta-initiatives that embed treasure into the practices, thought processes, and belief systems of an environment or culture. Along with administrative, strategic, verbal, cognitive, and logical initiatives that we prize in our organizations, *we must make room for values that honor, esteem, and celebrate the joy of God*—giving people permission to connect with joy and make room for it in new and powerful ways. Celebrating structural systems, strategy, and attainable goals only does not build or encourage a culture that results in a pervading atmosphere of abundant joy. What we celebrate—value, esteem, and make room for—ultimately shapes a culture.

It stands to reason that God is attracted to individuals, families, churches, and organizations in which He can see Himself reflected. Meaning, they have made room for His values, His ways, and His nature into the fabric of their DNA. The following are suggestions of culture shapers that may nurture increased joy:

- Cultivating places where God can be Himself.
- Gathering around the "It is finished" of the total and complete victory of Jesus.
- Modeling a culture of generosity and giving.
- Celebrating and honoring what God has done and is doing.
- Making room for ongoing personal renewal.
- Engaging in extravagant and extended worship of who He is.
- Developing structure that makes room for the interruptions of God.
- Creating environments that cultivate a constant attitude of learning.
- Nurturing environments of creativity that interpret and reflect the beauty and joy of God.
- Allowing a culture of permission to dream with God, and the imagining of joy-filled possibilities.
- Celebrating values that incubate and activate solutions cultivated from the heart of our joyful God.
- Giving permission for joy, laughter, delight, and wonder toward God and others.
- Encouraging a culture that promotes and grows capacity to return to joy authentically.

- A celebration of mindsets that embrace transformation, redemptive thinking, and expected upgrades.

- Providing places where there is room for a complete bandwidth of all gifts, callings, and anointings.

- Establishing a culture that celebrates joy in equal measure to productivity and excellence.

- Encouraging environments where joy capacity and receiving is maximized and diversions are minimized.

- Creating life-giving structures that are flexible so that chaos is avoided but control is minimized.

The concept of expanding and cultivating cultures that have the potential to nurture and release joy is an exciting one. God is the original Creator of culture and endues us with the same ability to imagine and shape environments that reflect Him. We are designed to rebuild, renew, and restore what does not yet look like Him or His ways. Jesus did not die only for individual salvation, but for societal transformation. Not from top down, but from the bottom up. This is an essential truth as we begin to move into shaping culture and bringing transformation.

Jesus said that those who wished to be the greatest in the Kingdom of Heaven would be the least; and unlike the world's system that dominates over others, leaders in His Kingdom would be servants of all.[28] What does it mean to be least? And what does it mean to serve? And, what does this have to do with joy and atmosphere? I am so glad you asked. Walking as least, is not a self-hating posture of unworthiness, but a recognition of the invitation to host the One who is most. It is a hosting posture that says let my personal agenda, priorities, and purpose become not only secondary, but subservient to Jesus and His manifest presence.

Servanthood comes in when we do this for the benefit of others. A maximizing of servanthood is delivering what Jesus the King is serving to lift, heal, forgive, restore, beautify, deliver, and love those who need it. How better than to do this by brokering the Father's presence so that they see Him much more than us, and experience what He has tailor-made for them in His infinite wisdom and purpose.

We are designed to host the manifest presence of God personally, corporately, and see it flow into every sphere of society. From the beginning, His desire to dwell with us has been the priority of His purpose. He moves us from *individual joy to corporate environments that multiply joy for others*. Change the atmosphere one moment at a time. Bring Heaven. Bring joy.

• • •

REDISCOVERING JOY: STEP 8

Engage in Prayer

> *Father, I thank You for all that You are and because of who You are, the heavenly reality is available to us as those who are Yours and seated with You. I love the atmosphere of Your presence that marks my life with love, joy, peace, and kindness, and overflows everywhere I go. Let*

personal revival and renewal be a distinctive mark upon my life—experiencing and cultivating dimensions of your presence, making room for an environment where You love to be Yourself. Create environments through me—a culture that begins with me and in me—and then beyond me to impact and shape my sphere of influence so that the transformation You are bringing is realized, and joy is manifest. I want to be a broker of heavenly realities, and a life that Your river moves through so that "everything will live." I upgrade my previous experience of what I have seen You do, for more, so that impossibilities become normal and the unreasonable becomes reasonable. Define my life by Your presence, Your very atmosphere, so that in hosting You, You define the very atmosphere around my life. Let a world that is waiting to be reminded of who You are and ready to discover who they are, crash into You and everything that You are.

Reflection

- Reflect on Revelation chapters 4, 5, 21, and 22. What impacts you about the atmosphere and reality of Heaven? When Jesus taught us to pray "on earth as it is in Heaven," He intended for all of this to be experienced on earth, in our reality. Lean into a fresh experience of God's atmosphere and ask Him to speak to you about His presence. Write down any pictures, visions, or encounters that He gives you.

- Take time to think about the factors that shape culture (the prayers that we pray, the stories that we tell, etc.). Think about the priority that you give these in your own journey and the culture that is being shaped by these factors. Is the outcome you are currently experiencing what you were expecting? Talk with God about what can be different going forward.

- Consider all of the spheres of influence in your own life, from immediate family, to friendships, workplace, church, and beyond. What is the Father laying on your heart to initiate or facilitate that will help shape an environment that will bring transformation and multiply joy?

Activation

- Identify your current phase in the process of moving into a joy-filled culture. Implement what God is asking and leading in order to upgrade where you are and move to the next step.

- Make room for two of the culture shaper suggestions at the end of the chapter and step out in creating space for them in your life, relationships, or schedule.

9

Invincible Joy

There is an incredible pattern in Scripture linking joy to victory. Of course in a natural sense, winning over something that has resisted God in our lives naturally releases joy and celebration in us. However, as God's image bearers and joy bearers we are hardwired to overcome, and the outworking of the release of God's Kingdom purposes releases great joy and fulfillment deep within us. This joy signals to us that we have partnered with God on something important to Him—and we resonate, not with a human joy or simply joy in our soul, but a deep, inexpressible joy that cannot be manufactured or replicated. It is almost as if God cheers us on with deposits of His joy that say, "Yes!" to our partnership with Him, that speak to the "well done" at the deepest parts of us.

The truth is, we were created to partner with the God of joy who is *the* Conqueror over darkness and all that keeps humanity bound and distant from Him.

> *The king rejoices in your strength, LORD. How great is his joy in the victories you give!* (Psalm 21:1 NIV)

In this simple line of praise and thanks in Psalm 21, we see a marriage between the concepts of strength, joy, and victory—a powerful picture of Jesus Himself, and also *us*, as those who are called and empowered to partner with Him over the stewardship of earth. The blending of these three powerful realities—strength, victory, joy—can be found as a running theme throughout Scripture; whether stated implicitly or only implied, the outworking of these heavenly attributes appear time and again in the great narrative of God's story.

As we truly begin to live fully alive in the Heaven-to-earth mandate of influencing our world in partnership with the Kingdom of God, we will draw upon, cooperate with, and become these very God attributes. Joy, strength, and victory are designed to perfectly fit us as God's people. Some parts of the church family believe that this sounds too lofty. Too proud. Maybe even dangerous. But God has amazing ways of helping us know that it's not us who has it all, and wonderful ways of helping us remember that we are flesh and blood indwelt by a supernatural, incredible, all-powerful Father. Those who have become new creations who bring His new creation to everywhere and everyone He sends us.

> *Then he said to them, "...this day is holy to our Lord. Do not sorrow, for the joy of the LORD is your strength"* (Nehemiah 8:10).
>
> *Then [Ezra] told them, "...this day is holy to our Lord. And be not grieved and depressed, for the joy of the Lord is your strength and stronghold"* (Nehemiah 8:10 AMPC).

In revealing His ways, God opens up for us understanding that it is *His joy that is actually our strength*. We know that wisdom, character, courage, and perseverance are all welcome as we advance the Kingdom, but God gives us a key for great strength in pointing us toward an unlikely weapon—His joy. Again, in order for the "joy of the Lord" to exist, by default it has to be resident in Him, and His desire for us to walk in His joy is evidenced by the fact that He gives it away to us. Joy then, is one of the foundational building blocks of our strength, and ultimately our victory. We tend to focus, quite rightly, on guarding the peace that He gives us. But if joy is linked to victory and to strength, *wisdom would have us also diligently guard and watch over the joy given to us by Holy Spirit.*

Because God says that His joy is our strength, we may want to reconsider how we have stewarded joy, and lift it out of the sidelines and shadows of insignificance and return it to its place among the list of fruit that God says we are to exhibit and display to reveal His nature through us as His sons and daughters.

Joy then is not the antithesis to strength as some may think, but is actually revealed as a powerful source of strength. It sounds just like the Father, whose strength is made perfect *in weakness*[1]— to require His joy to be the very basis of our strength. It is another paradox of the Kingdom that joy equals strength. But it does. Because He says so. When God reveals truth in His Word, He points us to His ways, but also provides an innate ability for the experiential fulfillment of that truth and promise to us. *He does not reveal the availability of something to us without providing the means for us to access it.* In revealing the truth that the joy of the

Lord is our strength, the Father is revealing a key to the way His Kingdom works, and a *benefit we are to access and live in.*

He also provides the opportunity for us to align by His Spirit, and enjoy and live in this intended joy that will become strength for us. He simply does not make promises without the backing of His character and power. Every piece of revealed truth in His Word is packed with wisdom that enables us access to the Kingdom in new ways. Exploring dimensions of the Kingdom of God is actually part of our birthright.

England is famous for its gardens; many impressive manor houses and stately homes are enhanced by equally impressive landscaped gardens. They were made to be admired, to walk through, to experience, to enjoy. They welcome us to step onto the terra firma and spend time soaking up the beauty of the curated detailed space. We *could* simply look at these gardens through the wrought iron gates that guard their entrance, peering through the bars, just enough to get a glimpse from one limited perspective.

This is how we often relate to many aspects of God's Kingdom, satisfied to glimpse through the railings as observers, not sure if we have the whole picture, or if we are taking away everything that we need. Maybe not believing we have an all-access pass, that the beauty of this garden is *not really for us.* Maybe reserved for a special class of person? Whereas in reality, we do not realize that we have permission to walk through the already unlocked gates to fully access what is already available to us; that which was meticulously and extravagantly designed, laid out, maintained, and presented generation after generation for our enjoyment, and to be *experienced.*

We have already been given the Kingdom. Let's walk into every place and dimension that the Father has made available to us. We need to increasingly explore and occupy every facet of the Father's domain—including His amazing joy and strength—if we are to truly possess our birthright and influence all that we are created to influence.

The world's systems insist that there are *more certain things* than joy that should function as our primary source of strength—giftings, wealth, position, intellectual capacity, counseling—all of which can be incredible assets to us when engaged healthily. But God loves to reveal unexpected and often uncomfortable truths that require faith in Him to lean into and are only dependent on Him to perform. This is true regarding the joy of the Lord being our strength. It is His, it comes from Him, and it is made available to us. The bottom line is, we must avoid leaning into any resource for strength that may only sustain us for a limited time.

Ultimately, the Father is jealous for us and desires that no other inferior master rule over us. Remember, He will often answer us according to our idols (see Ezekiel 14:4) because His goodness requires that we are never slaves to a lesser god. He desires His joy to be our strength because it is a superior Master to anything else we could use as a substitute for temporary strength. He is Father and Friend, and His ways never bring us into bondage, but always into fullness and our greatest potential. There is an invitation then to lean into the fullness of joy He has made available to us so we can be furnished with the kind of strength required to fulfill our fullest role.

When King David is faced with one of the most grueling challenges of his life (1 Samuel 30)— his wives and children captured, the village burned, and his men ready to kill him—he strengthens himself in the Lord.[2] It's not clear in Scripture exactly what this entails, but we know that God called David a man after His own heart, and that David was a worshiper, and inquired of the Lord continually. I believe a significant component of this strengthening was returning to the joy of God. In the face of impossible odds, refocusing, recapturing, and re-leaning into the God kind of joy that released strength to David would ultimately enable him to recover all.

We are in need of recover-all moments in our lives, families, cities, and nations. In Psalm 30:1, David worships God as the One who did not let his foes rejoice over him. This is who God is for us also. He acts on our behalf so that our enemy can no longer return to stealing joy from us or by subduing and diminishing our function.

God has designed us to be permanently furnished with a joy that is not moved by circumstances, and not dependent or defined by what is happening around us; rather, it is fixed, steady, available, and constant. The fruit of the Spirit is resident in us, and is cultivated moment by moment, and given permission to rise in our lives based on the choices we make, to ultimately have final authority over our days. We have a choice to make room for it.

I understand that not everything that happens to us is joyful; in fact, life's challenges are extremely difficult, designed to steal from us, distract us, and deplete us of effectiveness. We have personally navigated a miscarriage, family death, friends killed and imprisoned for their faith in hostile countries, betrayal, walking with close friends whose marriages have failed, sickness, exhaustion, raising children, and having to drink bad coffee(!). You could easily add your own additions to this list. We live in a fallen world.

But God has provided joy as a *pathway to strength* for us. We are empowered internally by the very Spirit of God, and permanently furnished from the inside with catalytic equipment that not only allows us to simply survive, but to advance and subdue what does not look like or reflect God and His ways. *Joy is designed to be an explosive weapon, not merely light relief in the middle of a gloomy day.* Joy is a force that galvanizes strength inside us. The following Old Testament passage of Scripture captures the marrying of strength and joy. We will overcome with slingstones as God's arrow appears, roaring "as with wine" at the victories of Jesus!

> *Then the LORD will appear over them; his arrow will flash like lightning. The Sovereign LORD will sound the trumpet; he will march in the storms of the south, and the LORD Almighty will shield them. They will destroy and overcome with slingstones. They will drink and roar as with wine; they will be full like a bowl used for sprinkling the corners of the altar. The LORD their God will save his people on that day as a shepherd saves his flock. They will sparkle in his land like jewels in a crown. How attractive and beautiful they will be! Grain will make the young men thrive, and new wine the young women* (Zechariah 9:14-17 NIV).

Spheres of culture are crying out for those who will move in love and compassion, but also those who will move in *His joy and His strength.* Sentimental concern alone will not bring transformation or answers to the seemingly insurmountable problems of our generation. A God kind of love married to a God kind of joy-strength will. Because the joy of the Lord is our strength, we must personally find our way back to joy, as David did, so that our strength is vibrant, replenished, and overflowing. Then turn to recover all on behalf of our communities and cities. There is always enough for us, and enough to give away.

Again, knowing that we are not called to be a self-serving pool but an overflowing river reminds us to check our water levels. Pausing to realize when we don't have enough for ourselves in a given area is a significant step for us in responding to reality. It is actually wisdom to recognize that we are depleted in any given area, so we can turn and be led back to the Source. God the magnificent, self-sustaining, radiant-Himself wants to train us by His Spirit how to return to joy at any given moment, in any circumstance so that our strength is permanent, and our strength is maximized.

My suggestion is that we make a decision ahead of time, to *choose joy* as a default no matter what comes, and then find our strength returning so that we can pivot and overcome whatever has come to take us out. Truthfully, yesterday will not return and tomorrow is not yet here. All we have is today. What will you choose? A joy-depleted, strength-depleted existence where your life is gradually stolen between the regrets of yesterday and the worries of tomorrow? Or a daily walk marked by choosing Him— and with Him, His joy, strength, hope, life, power, and victory.

Remember, His Kingdom is the Kingdom of righteousness, peace, and joy. It's part of your inheritance. To this He is adding strength that comes unconventionally and unexpectedly through returning to joy.

JOY AUTHORITY

Psalm 2 is a fierce declaration over nations and kingdoms found in the Old Testament narrative, and it reveals dimensions of the overcoming rule of Jesus as the One who has been set in place as the undisputed King over the earth. This is the reality that we are privileged to live in right now, the pronouncement that we live under, and the edict that we are to declare. The "It is finished." Jesus came demonstrating His Father's Kingdom and dealt with sin and death through His own sacrifice and blood, rose from the dead, and is now seated above all rule and authority in this age or the age to come releasing power to those who are His to do what He did—revealing the Father and bringing Heaven to earth.

The opening of Psalm 2 asks a still-echoing question, "Why do the nations rage?" There is an abundance of unrest, tumult, and rage in our world—in our communities, cities, and often in our own hearts. Offense, anger, and frustration are hungry, even greedy for our attention and alliance. It's Christianity 101, isn't it? The choice to lean into our old disempowered nature is always before us, with Galatians 5:19 saying clearly that "the works of the flesh are evident."

Scripture also teaches that the mind set on the flesh is death, but the mind set on the Spirit is life and peace.[3] We live in the moment-by-moment choice of what will capture our attention and allegiance, and whether we will walk in life, peace, and joy— or death, confusion, and anxiety.

In the middle of the nations' raging and kings throwing off the rule of God, the psalmist states something quite wonderful:

The One enthroned in heaven laughs... (Psalm 2:4).

Let's re-read that verse a number of times so that it penetrates our hearts and minds. We have been discovering in a new way that God sings over us. But He also laughs. As the Church, we have not focused on the posture and positioning of God in the middle of international chaos when the nations rage. Instead, we are pulled and pushed, manipulated by every opinion, perspective, and pronouncement that comes into our vision or within our hearing.

Taking a moment to see how *He is responding* may be the key to the Body of Christ overcoming the momentous flood of seemingly negative outcomes in our world. The nations rage; and God laughs. Not an uncaring callous laugh, but a victorious ruling laugh over the plans of darkness that lie behind so much unrest. There are incredibly intense situations, and as I have shared in my involvement with the persecuted Church, there is loss, deep sadness, and pain as we pursue the Kingdom. But incredibly, the God who laughs has the ultimate perspective, and the final word on all that is happening in our world.

> *...He said to me, "You are my son, today I have become your father. Ask me, and I will make the nations your inheritance, the ends of the earth your possession"* (Psalm 2:8 NIV).

This is an amazing Scripture to fuel intercession, and I love to ask the Father for the nations. But sometimes we ask for the nations as servants, or even friends of God, both of which are truths. However, He is upgrading us to live in the reality that *only sons can ask for an inheritance within the hearing of the laugh of the Father.* We are not only those who ask for nations in order to serve them, but we ask for nations as *part of the family inheritance and the Father's story.* This adjustment significantly alters our approach, motive, and the authority from which we will operate. The heart's desire of a son or daughter outweighs even the most honorable service of a servant. We are being transformed by the renewing of our minds.

I want you to catch this, because it is under the pronouncement of the laugh of God that His children have permission to ask for nations as an inheritance in the Father's eternal story. *In the context of the Father's laugh, the rage of nations receives its boundary.* It is the atmosphere of the Father's joy that sets the tone, the pulse, and the mandate in our fight for our communities—dethroning rage, restlessness, and rebellion. Unmoved and unmandated by the rage of nations and rulers, both natural and spiritual, God has set Jesus in place, who is now seated.[4] The ultimate victory through the ultimate Son—*Christus Victor*—the One who *has already* won, and who has the final word.

Living and operating under the laugh of the Father is our inheritance. Allowing the joy of God to lead the dance from a spark into a raging fire is the answer to rage and restlessness from the smallest seed in our own heart soil, to the biggest announcements of chaos in the nations. *The One enthroned in heaven laughs.* Joy permeates the halls of Heaven and joy is to permeate the process of the destiny of nations.

Ephesians chapter 1 informs us of the current cosmic reality, and tells us that according to His good pleasure, God is bringing everything in Heaven and earth under one head, who is Christ.

In the context of His laugh and good pleasure, God positions us to be partners in seeing all things in Heaven and earth being gathered up under Christ's headship:

> *...With all wisdom and understanding, he made known to us the mystery of his will according to his good pleasure, which he purposed in Christ, to be put into effect when the times reach their fulfillment—to bring unity to all things in heaven and on earth under Christ* (Ephesians 1:8-10 NIV).

Other translations of this passage state: "gather together in one all things," "re-establish all things," and "sum up all things" in Christ.[5] As we have discussed, this will happen through individuals who will walk as disciples, creating environments, and organizational cultures—biospheres that are saturated and marked by joy, releasing Heaven's values and authority and bringing transformation.

Jesus gave the Church operational authority when He conferred on us the keys of the Kingdom:

> *And Jesus answered him, "...on this rock I will build my church, and the gates of hell shall not prevail against it. I will give you the keys of the kingdom of heaven, and whatever you bind on earth shall be bound in heaven, and whatever you loose on earth shall be loosed in heaven"* (Matthew 16:17-19 ESV).

The Church functions simultaneously in several dimensions; it is a family, an army, a representation of Heaven, and a governing counsel to name some. The word *ekklesia* is used here by Jesus to describe the Church.[6] It is profound that He uses a nonreligious term meaning a called-out governing council or assembly. Along with the term *apostle,* which was also a secular term, meaning sent one,[7] delegate, or ambassador (whose function was to make the conquered culture look like the conqueror's), creating a powerful picture for us of the vested authority given to the early church leaders and the Church. It is also applicable to us today and the corporate authority we carry as the Church along with its leadership. We are *sent* communities who govern, represent Heaven, and shape the culture of earth to look like Heaven, all in the context of servant, friendship, kingship as outlined earlier.

As stewards of environments that cultivate and multiply joy, we use the keys of authority to release the joy that is inherent in God, under the laugh of Heaven, to see the systems of nations come and experience change. As much as individual discipleship remains crucial to this process, Jesus' mandate to the Church was to disciple *nations* (Matthew 28:19), which infers a rebuilding, renewal, and restoration of their structures, systems, and infrastructure, as well as individuals and churches.

We carry the solutions and the authority within us, and within the cultures that we shape, to bring the laugh of Heaven into a broken world that God is already in the process of restoring. The invincible joy of God is part of the invincible restoration. We were not made to do it without it.

• • •

REDISCOVERING JOY: STEP 9

Engage in Prayer

> *Father, You have created me to be marked and totally saturated by strength, victory, and joy. There are cultural realities that are claiming to be invincible, attempting to shout louder than Your solutions and love to intimidate Your sons and daughters. Thank You for the greater yes, the "It is finished," and the strength that is mobilized through the presence of Your joy. Alert me to guard the reserves of joy that You are giving, so that my strength is renewable and available for every fight. Thank You that the rage of nations receives its boundaries underneath Your laugh, and as Your children we get to ask for our inheritance underneath the presence of Your joy and laughter over the earth. Your joy is my strength. Release Your laugh through me as a delegated carrier of Your authority to the systems, infrastructure, and cultures of this world. Thank You for invincible joy.*

Reflection

- Reflect on the level of strength you are experiencing in certain areas. Ask the Father how He wants to refresh you and replenish Your strength. Have you leaned out of His joy in the last season? What is He showing you about accessing it again?
- Think about what areas are resisting the reality of the Kingdom in your own life, or the lives of those around you. At the core of the issue, what does

darkness want to gain in stealing this from you or from those you love? Receive strategic answers and joyful strength to reclaim and recover what Jesus is doing in that circumstance.

- Meditate on Christ the overcomer—Christus Victor—and all that this means for our world. Colossians 1:15-21 and Revelation 19:11-21 carry powerful revelation.

Activation

- Pray into the rage that is in the nations by asking God to release His laugh according to Psalm 2. Watch as He moves and silences the chaos with His joy. Ask Him for nations as Your inheritance as a son or daughter. Pray over your city and neighborhood in the same way.

- Take steps to bring any area of your life under submission to the joy of God, and the "It is finished" of the cross and resurrection. Hear and receive the laugh of the Father over every place of anxiety, pain, offense, or worry. Let it go and let God be God.

10

The Final Laugh

*Arise [from the depression and prostration in which
circumstances have kept you—rise to a new life]! Shine
(be radiant with the glory of the Lord), for your light
has come, and the glory of the Lord has risen upon you.*
—Isaiah 60:1 AMPC

*T*his is an arise-and-shine moment. Some of the greatest places of God's radiance emerge out of the places of the deepest and darkest turmoil. He is the Master of the impossible turnaround. The Message translation of the Bible says, "...Put your face in the sunlight. GOD's bright glory has risen for you." How much brighter can it get than an eternal, forever-established, immovable "It is finished" over sin, sickness, hell, principalities and powers, death, and the grave—and an empowered Church filled with resurrection life by God Himself?

What the cross purchased and the resurrection sealed, the Spirit in us brings to life and releases through us. What the resurrection sealed, the Spirit reveals. What the cross purchased, the Spirit propagates. Just as in the genesis of creation, Holy Spirit still broods over chaotic, barren, dead places waiting for the "let there be light" from the Father.[1] The truth is that the Father has already spoken through His Son, and the "It is finished" resonates throughout the universe.

The born-again experience marks the beginning of a journey, not the end, and is full of Heaven's possibilities as we also resonate with this same sound—bringing Heaven to transform the earth, rather than simply longing to escape earth for Heaven's reality. The current reality of what He has already done, who we are in Him, and who He is in us is actually the incarnation of joy itself. This is the joy of God lived out. This is the joy of God forever established. The joy of God seen and manifest. The end goal. His plan all along.

SUMMARY

In attempting to reframe and re-present joy to you, we have explored various dimensions, starting with God the Source and His deposits of joy-causing brilliance and beauty that we can easily find in creation. Irresistible to us and wonder filled, we find joy kindled in us through seeing Him in all that He has made. It is wonderful to us. Jesus, the Son anointed "with the oil of joy"[2] revealing the Father, doing remarkably kind and gracious miracles that exploded joy upon the undeserving and oppressed, and on all who looked on in amazement. Too good to be true—but exceedingly true.

The Kingdom of joy and the roar of the Spirit of God at Pentecost releasing upon the unsuspecting, ragtag, unqualified disciples an authority, an anointing, and a commissioning to do "even greater works" than Jesus.[3] Mind blowing. We looked at the indwelling presence of Holy Spirit as our interface to the Father, and the inside-out manifestation of the God kind of joy through our lives, and into our world—so we are not only carriers of joy, but dispensers of the answers that bring it unreservedly and without cost into the lives of those around us. Carriers. Conduits. Brokers. We live in a permanent invitation for a permanent flow of life into every dead place.

We discussed recognizing the potential for things that can diminish our joy, and identifying a navigation plan to avoid and remove the influence of them in our lives; the enigmatic surprise of scientific research and brain science; and the confirmation of the Father's call for us to return to joy. Finishing with discussion about environments and cultures that multiply and carry the pervading atmosphere of joy to bring a rebuilding, restoration, renewal to the infrastructure, systems, and spheres of society, as well as the authority that joy carries as an ongoing source of our strength to overcome for those who ask Him for nations under the sound of His laughter.

We talked in the opening of the book about the importance of the lenses of transformation, redemption, and expected upgrades to the process of reclaiming and increasing joy. It is exciting now to view what has been laid out for us, regarding the power of joy, *through these lenses*, to see possibilities and potential that may have not been visible before.

When all has been said, what can argue with unpredictable, authentic, raw, unrehearsed joy when it appears? God, in just being Himself has created joy as part of our world and our experience, simply to be enjoyed, and in turn, for Him to delight in us enjoying joy. We all resonate with the presence of contagious joy when something amazing happens for someone we love and care for. Joy is to be enjoyed!

If you remember nothing else, know that joy is an attribute of our amazing Father just being Himself. His kindness, love, and power touching places that have been ravished by darkness and depravity and brings unrealistic restoration by the world's standards. The good news is better than we think, more wonderful than we have allowed. And when someone is touched by restoration and life, they cannot help but respond with joy—and we respond with them. The Father is spreading His joy today, just like He always has done. The Architect Father has planned a way for His joy to not only be resident in those who are His, but unleashed upon a fallen world groaning for the echo of the joy of God to be heard in their ears, and inside their souls.

God's solution was His Son, and sons of God who are now revealed,[4] showing up in every realm of society carrying the God-kind of joy that awakens a distant memory for the pre-saved, of who they are *supposed to be*. The joy of God becomes a beacon, a lighthouse, a Wi-Fi signal in the everyday hum and intensity of what *really matters*. It's a rallying call, a summoning, a flare that invades with joy from another realm. It breaks through monotony, pain, and dullness bringing a spark from the Creator that awakens the dead places and lives that are dying.

The laugh of Heaven released into our world reminds us of the Father who began everything with His indelible sparkling light. The invincible joy of God has spoken from eternity past and into eternity future and is a fierce proclamation of total and *complete restoration*. That which ignited joy in the angelic hosts at the creation of the world is still at work—it comes at times like an explosive projectile, and at times like a feather-whisper into our hearts as the Father begins to awaken us to wonder.

So, let it come with a surge into our communities; let it spread like a wild unstoppable thunderous force that multiplies, resonates, and shouts to all of the goodness of God and His ridiculously kind restorative heart that brings life, hope, and new beginnings to everything He touches.

Double-dosed places of trouble and shame and seeming defeat become the resourced places of redemption filled to the brim with joy, favor, and hope that speaks to "arise and shine." He wants to literally surprise and apprehend people with the power of the joy that is resting on your life and in the environment that surrounds you:

> *Return to your stronghold, O prisoners of hope; today I declare that I will restore to you double* (Zechariah 9:12 ESV).
>
> *But you will be known as Priests of Yahweh and called Servants of our God. You will feast on the wealth of nations and revel in their riches! Because you received a double dose of shame and dishonor, you will inherit a double portion of endless joy and everlasting bliss!* (Isaiah 61:6-7 TPT)

The very details of your past defeats are the invitations for solutions and strongholds of hope for someone else's journey. The blueprints behind every enemy assignment is intimately known to you, because you have lived it. Our lives have been restored to how things should be—all of the "dis" places being returned to creation design. Dis-ease to health. Dis-repair to restoration. Dis-honor to honor. Dis-empowerment to powerful identity. Dis-contentment to fulfillment.

We are qualified and gain authority in every place we overcome. We were made for problems—"solutionaries"—who bring joyful solutions from Heaven into this realm. The systems, environments, and culture that God allows us to shape in our own lives, families, churches, and organizations carry a pervading atmosphere of His joy that floods darkness with nowhere to remain.

The Kingdom of righteousness, peace, and joy that we have learned so much about, champions the removal of pain, torment, and depression—everything opposite to the nature of God. It is pro-joy. Everything about the Kingdom moves to annihilate hindrances to joy and promotes joy into the fabric of the lives of people. Everywhere the river goes, everything will live.[5] I want to keep repeating this until it saturates our thinking and our motivation and our expectation. Everything. Will. Live.

It is my personal conviction that there is much to keep us occupied this side of Heaven, and many assignments to fulfill before we can say that all things have been gathered together in Christ.[6] We owe the world a glimpse of the joyful Father who planned a love relationship with them before the beginning of time. The world has seen a principled church, a hypocritical church at times, a preaching church, a caring church—but what about a 21st-century joy-filled Church that loves sacrificially, walks in the power of Heaven, and brings solutions to problems that people cannot fix. A Church full of people who are unmistakably marked by the joy and bliss of the Father—unapologetically loved, unreasonably joyful, and remarkably generous. I think a world is waiting for people like this.

> *On this mountain the LORD of hosts will make for all peoples a feast of rich food, a feast of well-aged wine, of rich food full of marrow, of aged wine well refined. And he will swallow up on this mountain the covering that is cast over all peoples, the veil that is spread over all nations. He will swallow up death forever; and the Lord GOD will wipe away tears from all faces, and the reproach of his people he will take away from all the earth, for the LORD has spoken* (Isaiah 25:6-8 ESV).

The feast of His presence, and the feast of His joy are already here. Death, the shroud that covered all people, has been swallowed up forever—and provision has been made for tears to be wiped away from all faces, not just in a future age, but here and now. From the Garden to Revelation, and this epoch in-between where we find ourselves, the story begins and ends with joy.

The book of Revelation carries descriptive encounters of Heaven's joy and the reality of the atmosphere that surrounds the Father being Himself. This is where the incredible final marriage feast of the Lamb will take place at the end of the ages, when everything is concluded.

Our focus is not to be *the end* because so much vision fills us for transformation possibilities in *the now*. Rather, we are to live fueled by the same joy that exists in Heaven's realm. Our environments and culture are to emanate with the culture of Heaven. The nations were made ultimately to shine in joy and find their fulfillment free of fear, death, sorrow, and pain. The picture painted for us in Heaven carries the power of invincible joy, marking for us how things *should be* when the Father's joy pervades.

The anticipation, celebration, and festivity of a cosmic wedding is in our DNA. We are being prepared for the most joyful celebration in history—where the final rewards of Christ's suffering and the perseverance of the Church will be fulfilled.

> *Let us be glad and rejoice and give Him glory, for the marriage of the Lamb has come, and His wife has made herself ready* (Revelation 19:7).

The God and Father of the end and the beginning saw the joy of final restoration as He made plans for our redemption. All this before the foundation of the world.[7] His joy was in motion and stirring as He marked the overarching narrative of history—starting with the beauty of the Garden and ending with the wedding of His Son. His own joyful mandate to rebuild, renew, and restore all things finds its beginning and end in Himself. Joyful anticipation stirs in me to hear the song and the laughter of God—the joyful Architect of all His-story, at the wedding of His Son.

He who was seated on the throne said, "I am making everything new!" Then he said, "Write this down, for these words are trustworthy and true." He said to me: "It is done. I am the Alpha and Omega, the Beginning and the End. To the thirsty I will give water without cost from the spring of the water of life. Those who are victorious will inherit all this, and I will be their God and they will be my children (Revelation 21:5-7 NIV).

• • •

REDISCOVERING JOY: STEP 10

Engage in Prayer

God, I choose to arise and shine, at this time, in the place of purpose You have positioned me. We owe the world an encounter with You, the joyful Father who awakens us to wonder in everything that He does. Out of expectation of the greatest joy celebration in history, use me to call individuals, spheres of culture, systems, and infrastructure into the rebuilding, renewal, and restoration that You are initiating. Let the intimacy of the Garden and the joy of the wedding feast of Jesus be abundantly evident on my lips and on my face now, from this moment on. I want to be a carrier of the last laugh. Expecting wonder. Expecting light. Expecting transformation. A laugh that is louder than every place of dread, despair, and darkness. God, You are the everlasting, uncaused, self-existent One, the self-sufficient, self-sustaining, luminous, radiant One. Making everything new.

Reflection

- Reflect on the chapters of the book, and the journey you have taken from being introduced to the God of Joy, to the One who laughs over the nations. What has impacted you most powerfully? If you haven't already, journal any revelation you are taking with you.

- Think about what it means to carry the permanent presence of the last laugh, knowing that He has won, and good ultimately wins. Let the reality of this saturate you and your expectations of the future. What would it mean to truly be a prisoner of hope? (See Zechariah 9:12.)

- Take some time to ponder eternity with the Father. It's going to be inexplicably amazing, and gloriously joyful. Forever.

Activation

- Return to joy every moment of every day, no matter what comes.

- Laugh more than you ever have before.

Endnotes

CHAPTER I

1. Cited in the *Westminster Shorter Catechism* dated 1646-1647.
2. Luke 11:1-5.
3. Genesis 2:15.
4. Revelation 19:9.
5. Hebrews 12:2.
6. Revelation 21:4.
7. Romans 5:2.
8. 2 Timothy 1:14.
9. Nehemiah 8:10.
10. Ecumenical councils recognized by both Eastern Orthodox and Roman Catholics and the year of the council: First Council of Nicaea (325); First Council of Constantinople (381); Council of Ephesus (431); Council of Chalcedon (451); Second Council of Constantinople (553); Third Council of Constantinople (680–681); Second Council of Nicaea (787); cited in the *Encyclopaedia Britannica;* https://www.britannica .com/topic/council-Christianity; accessed July 6, 2020.
11. Revelation 2:7,17; 3:22.

12. Examples of these include: Elijah House, Coeur d'Alene, Idaho, USA, www.elijahhouse.org; Restoring The Foundations, Mount Juliet, Tennessee, USA, www.restoringthefoundations .org; Transformed Hearts Ministries, Post Falls, Idaho, USA, www.transformedheartsministries.org; Sozo, Redding, California, USA, www.bethelsozo.com.
13. 2 Corinthians 10:13-15.
14. John 15:11.
15. John 5:6.
16. Philippians 3:14.
17. Genesis 1:26-28; Luke 4:18-19; Mark 16:15-19; Matthew 28:19-20.
18. Acts 17:6.
19. Isaiah 61:3 NIV.
20. Luke 4:18-19.
21. Isaiah 53:5.
22. Genesis 1:3.
23. Luke 2:14.

CHAPTER 2

1. Hebrews 11:3 NIV: *"By faith we understand that the universe was formed at God's command, so that what is seen was not made out of what was visible."*
2. 2 Corinthians 4:18 NIV: *"So we fix our eyes not on what is seen, but on what is unseen, since what is seen is temporary, but what is unseen is eternal."*
3. Psalm 23:4.
4. Isaiah 40:15.
5. Genesis 1:3.
6. 1 Peter 1:19-20.
7. The National Archives; http://www.nationalarchives.gov.uk/ latin/stage-1-latin/resources/stage-1-latin-grammar-resource/ prepositions/; accessed July 7, 2020.
8. Ephesians 2:10.

9. Ezekiel 16:4-14.
10. Romans 8:15.
11. 1 Corinthians 13:8.
12. Ephesians 3:19.

CHAPTER 3

1. Leviticus 25:10.
2. Mark 1:40.
3. Luke 5:17.
4. John 8:1-11.
5. Luke 7:11-17.
6. Luke 8:43.
7. Luke 5:26; Acts 2:43; Luke 1:65; Mathew 9:8.
8. Luke 15:11-32.
9. *agalliaō*, Strong's G21; and *gîyl*, Strong's H1523; Psalm 13:5.
10. Hebrews 12:2 AMPC.
11. John 16:7.

CHAPTER 4

1. Matthew 6:10; 16:19.
2. John 14:12.
3. Genesis 1:26-28; Luke 4:18-19; Mark 16:15-19; Matthew 28:19-20.
4. Philippians 2:9.
5. "We reflect in darkness what we are called to in light." –Pastor Bill Johnson, Bethel Church, Redding, CA.
6. John 10:10.

CHAPTER 5

1. Ephesians 3:20 NIV.
2. Merriam-Webster; https://www.merriam-webster.com/dictionary/abide.
3. Luke 10:38-42.

4. The apostle John was not negating the need for teachers; he was speaking to disciples who were healthily connected into the functioning Body of Christ and would have sat under teachers and preachers. He was highlighting the reality of the forever invitation of the indwelling Holy Spirit as The Teacher within every believer.
5. John 12:49; 5:19.
6. Ezekiel 47.
7. Ephesians 5:18.
8. Psalm 23:5.
9. Daniel 7:10; Revelation 20:12.
10. Revelation 6:9-11.
11. Hebrews 12:2.
12. 2 Corinthians 11:24-28.
13. 2 Corinthians 1:9.

CHAPTER 6

1. Ephesians 3:15.
2. Galatians 3:28.
3. 2 Corinthians 3:18.
4. Ezekiel 14:4.
5. John 4:24.
6. Ephesians 1:18 NIV.
7. Exodus 14:13; Matthew 10:22; Ephesians 6:14.
8. Psalm 23:3.
9. Galatians 6:2.
10. Contact information for recommended personal freedom ministries is listed in Chapter 1, Endnote 12. Licensed counselors and therapists can be located in your geographic area.
11. Ephesians 2:5-6.
12. 2 Corinthians 10:5.
13. 1 John 4:18.
14. John 10:10.

15. Colossians 2:15.
16. John 14:30.
17. John 8:36.
18. Emma Seppälä, "A Harvard professor explains why the world is actually becoming a much better place," *The Washington Post*, February 13, 2018. Dr. Steven Pinker states, "…rates of war have been roller-coastering downward since 1946, rates of American homicide have plunged since 1992, and rates of disease, starvation, extreme poverty, illiteracy and dictatorship, when they are measured by a constant yardstick, have all decreased—not to zero, but by a lot." Although Pinker cites the reason for this as a support-case for "enlightenment, humanism and reason," the facts remain that factors of doom are on the decrease, even with all of the difficulty in our world. https://www.washingtonpost.com/news/inspired-life/wp/2018/02/13/a-famed-harvard-professor-explains-why-the-world-is-actually-becoming-a-much-better-place/; accessed July 9, 2020.
19. Matthew 13:24,37.
20. Matthew 24:36.
21. Matthew 6:34.
22. Matthew 25:1-13.
23. 1 John 2:16.
24. James 1:13-15.
25. Luke 6:45.
26. Luke 6:37.
27. James 3:9-13.
28. Leviticus 23:1-44.
29. Matthew 11:19.

CHAPTER 7

1. Jon Meacham, "Free to Be Happy," *TIME* magazine, June 27, 2013; www.nation.time.com/2013/06/27/free-to-be-happy/print/; accessed April 20, 2020.

2. "The World Happiness Report 2019"; https://worldhappiness
.report/ed/2019/changing-world-happiness/; accessed July 18,
2020.

3. Megan Gibson, Kharunya Paramaguro, "The States of
Happiness," *TIME* magazine, July 8, 2013; https://nation.time
.com/2013/06/27/whos-happy-around-the-world/; accessed
July 18, 2020.

4. Ibid.

5. Jeffrey Kluger, "The Happiness of Pursuit," *TIME* magazine,
July 8, 2013; http://content.time.com/time/magazine/
article/0,9171,2146449,00.html; accessed July 9, 2020.

6. On The Brain, "Humor, Laughter, and Those Aha Moments,"
The Harvard Mahoney Neuroscience Institute Letter, Spring 2010;
https://hms.harvard.edu/sites/default/files/HMS_OTB
_Spring10_Vol16_No2.pdf; accessed April 20, 2020.

7. https://www.researchgate.net/publication/51645748_Social
_laughter_is_correlated_with_an_elevated_pain_threshold;
accessed April 20, 2020.

8. Kavita Khajuria, MD, "Laughter Is the Best Medicine,"
PsychiatricTimes, August 17, 2018; https://www
.psychiatrictimes.com/cultural-psychiatry/laughter-best
-medicine; accessed April 20, 2020.

9. Ibid.

10. Mayo Clinic Staff, "Stress relief from laughter? It's no joke,"
Mayo Clinic, April 5, 2019; https://www.mayoclinic.org/
healthy-lifestyle/stress-management/in-depth/stress-relief/art
-20044456; accessed April 20, 2020.

11. Ibid.

12. Ibid.

13. Ibid.

14. Ibid.

15. Ibid.

16. Ibid.

17. Kavita Khajuria, MD, "Laughter Is the Best Medicine,"
PsychiatricTimes, August 17, 2018; https://www

.psychiatrictimes.com/cultural-psychiatry/laughter-best -medicine; accessed April 20, 2020.

18. B. King, *Health-Related Benefits of Humor and Laughter.* Seminar DVDs. Los Banos, CA: Institute for Brain Potential; cited in "Laughter Is the Best Medicine," *PsychiatricTimes,* August 13, 2018.

19. N. Cousins, Anatomy of an Illness. NEJM. 1976:293:1458- 1463; cited in "Laughter Is the Best Medicine," *PsychiatricTimes,* August 17, 2018.

20. Khajuria, "Laughter Is the Best Medicine," *PsychiatricTimes,* August 17, 2018.

21. Ibid.

22. B. King, *Health-Related Benefits of Humor and Laughter;* cited in "Laughter Is the Best Medicine," *PsychiatricTimes,* August 17, 2018.

23. R.I.M. Dunbar, et.al., "Social laughter is correlated with an elevated pain threshold," *Proceedings of The Royal Society,* September 14, 2011; https://www.researchgate.net/ publication/51645748_Social_laughter_is_correlated_with _an_elevated_pain_threshold; accessed April 20, 2020.

24. Ibid.

25. Jeffrey Kluger, "The Happiness of Pursuit," *TIME* magazine, July 8, 2013; http://content.time.com/time/magazine/ article/0,9171,2146449,00.html; accessed July 9, 2020.

26. Ibid.

27. Emma Seppälä, "6 Secrets to a Happier Life," *TIME* magazine, August 7, 2017; https://time.com/4856944/secrets -happier-life/; accessed July 11, 2020.

28. Ibid.

29. Jeffrey Kluger, "The Happiness of Pursuit," *TIME* magazine, July 8, 2013; http://content.time.com/time/magazine/ article/0,9171,2146449,00.html; accessed July 11, 2020.

30. Ibid.

31. Ibid.

32. 1 Timothy 6:10.

33. Ellen Seidman, "Fourteen Ways to Jump for Joy," *TIME* Magazine, The Science of Happiness, Special Edition, 2016, page 36.
34. Ibid.
35. Bryan Walsh, "Does Spirituality Make You Happy?" *TIME* magazine; August 17; https://time.com/4856978/spirituality-religion-happiness/; accessed July 11, 2020.
36. Ibid.
37. Key concepts from this "Brain science" section were taken from a brain science seminar led by Dr. Marcus Warner at Sojourn Church, TX, June 20, 2019. Used with permission. For more information regarding Dr. Warner's work, visit www.DeeperWalkInternational.org

CHAPTER 8

1. The word *atmosphere* has been used intentionally here in order to help dislodge us from more familiar and commonly used words such as presence or anointing. This enables us to approach biblical truth through a slightly different lens.
2. Ezekiel 1:10-12, 16, 26-27.
3. Matthew 1:18-21; Matthew 2:13-23.
4. Acts 1; 3:1-11; Acts 5:1-17; Acts 8:9-15.
5. Colossians 1:16.
6. Revelation 21:23; 5:11; 17:14; 5:5; 8:3-6; 7:9-13; 21:4; 21:5.
7. John 3:3.
8. Ephesians 1:17.
9. John 5:19.
10. Revelation 4:1
11. John 15:15.
12. Jeremiah 1:4-5.
13. 1 Corinthians 12:10.
14. Several titles are interchangeable here, including revival movement or neo-charismatic movement.
15. Luke 11:3.

16. Acts 3:1-10.
17. John 14:12.
18. Acts 5:15.
19. Luke 8:43 KJV.
20. Luke 8:45-47.
21. 1 Samuel 10:5-13.
22. Ezekiel 47:9.
23. 2 Corinthians 2:15-17.
24. John 10:10.
25. Psalm 20:4.
26. Isaiah 61:4.
27. https://www.24-7prayer.com; accessed July 10, 2020.
28. Matthew 20:24-26.

CHAPTER 9

1. 2 Corinthians 12:9.
2. 1 Samuel 30:6.
3. Romans 8:6 NIV.
4. Psalm 2:6.
5. KJV; Douay-Rheims 1752 Revision; American Standard Version.
6. Strong's G1577.
7. Strong's G652.

CHAPTER 10

1. Genesis 1:1.
2. Hebrews 1:9 NIV.
3. John 14:12.
4. Romans 8:19.
5. Ezekiel 47.
6. Ephesians 1:10 KJV.
7. Revelation 13:8.

FREEDOM MINISTRIES MENTIONED

Elijah House, Coeur d'Alene, Idaho, USA, www.elijahhouse.org

Restoring The Foundations, Mount Juliet, Tennessee, USA, www.restoringthefoundations.org

Transformed Hearts Ministries, Post Falls, Idaho, USA, www.transformedheartsministries.org

Sozo, Redding, California, USA, www.bethelsozo.com

ABOUT ROLAND WORTON

Roland Worton has worked alongside churches, ministries, and conferences in cross-cultural and multi-generational settings for the last twenty-five years. He is currently part of the executive pastoral team at Sojourn Church in Dallas TX and is the founder of Soundforgers, an organization committed to the release of creative initiatives. Roland's assignment also includes working extensively in the Middle East with emerging underground church networks. Roland has been married to Shirin for twenty-three years, and they have two teenage sons.

Contact Information
Website: www.soundforgers.org

DESTINY IMAGE BOOKS BY ROLAND WORTON

Emerging Worship:
Becoming Part of the Sound and Song of Heaven